A GERMAN REVIEW GRAMMAR

A GERMAN REVIEW GRAMMAR

By T. HERBERT ETZLER
SOUTHERN METHODIST UNIVERSITY

and HARVEY I. DUNKLE
SAN DIEGO STATE COLLEGE

New York · THE ODYSSEY PRESS · INC·

PREFACE

We have found from our years of experience on various campuses that the second-year student desperately needs a thorough review of grammar and syntax, whether he intends to do advanced work in German, to use German materials in his own field of interest, or to make personal contact with speakers of German. We have therefore looked at the over-all arrangement of the subject matter from a fresh viewpoint and have arranged the material in a way which varies somewhat from that of other intermediate texts.

Verb forms, the logical and mechanical heart of any idea, are presented in alternate lessons so that all verb forms have been discussed by Lesson 10. It is obviously mere tradition, and of no particular significance, that subjunctive forms have been found last in review grammars, even though the second-year student is reading all verb forms in context from the beginning of his course.

Also, we have emphasized certain features of German which require the American student to acquire new ways of thinking. The reflexive pronoun and the uses of the genitive and dative cases are therefore treated in more detail than we have found elsewhere. We consider it self-evident that a student can learn the tables of adjective endings, for example, without any particular effort to understand the "why," because they are merely patterns of sound and rhythm that are acquired with a little practice. However, an

v

understanding of dative usage not depending on prepositions presents a real problem, which we have tried to deal with rationally because the American is conditioned to distinguishing only one "objective" case.

The types of oral exercises vary from lesson to lesson because different points of instruction require different kinds of practice. Thus the lists of nouns in the first two lessons familiarize the student with common nouns and verbs derived from the same roots while he is practicing the forms of nouns and verbs. Insertion exercises appear in Lessons 3 and 5, for example, because they are best suited to practice in choosing a specific form to fit a context. In Lessons 4 and 6, concerning verb forms, short statements for oral translation enable the student to test himself on the choice of form before he begins the written exercise. Sometimes, as in Lesson 7 on reflexive pronouns, oral exercises consist of illustrations which the student needs to study carefully as preparation for the written exercise. Each oral exercise was designed to accomplish a particular purpose appropriate to the lesson; the result is a variety of exercises without a stereotyped format. Also, the quantity of oral exercises varies, depending on the amount or complexity of other material in the lesson. The length of each lesson is such that it can be assigned for one class period.

The written exercises, designed to test the student's mastery of the lesson, are consistent in quantity except that the early lessons contain shorter and simpler sentences. A gradual increase in complexity seems to be an obvious requirement here.

The decision not to include readings will meet, we hope, with the approval of most teachers. Grammars containing excerpts of stories cause two kinds of frustration: the excerpts are no substitute for the complete stories, and the correlation of the lesson to the excerpt is no greater than it would be to any other reading. Furthermore, we do not want to interfere with the teacher's freedom to select his favorite readings.

As a whole, we view this text as serving two purposes: first, to accomplish the systematic review customary in a second-year course; and, second, to provide a reference book for the student's later use. To satisfy the second need, a detailed index and various appendices have been added.

CONTENTS

LESSON 1

DER-WORDS, EIN-WORDS, AND NOUNS IN THE SINGULAR

---

1) Declension of Nouns with der-words

The **der-**words are the definite article and

dieser	this	**mancher**	many (a)
jener	that	**solcher**	such (a)
jeder	each, every	**welcher**	which, what (a)

	M.	M.	F.	N.	N.
N.	der Tisch	dieser Wagen	welche Uhr	das Haus	jedes Zimmer
G.	des Tisches	dieses Wagens	welcher Uhr	des Hauses	jedes Zimmers
D.	dem Tisch(e)	diesem Wagen	welcher Uhr	dem Haus(e)	jedem Zimmer
A.	den Tisch	diesen Wagen	welche Uhr	das Haus	jedes Zimmer

Masculine and neuter nouns regularly have **–s** or **–es** in the genitive singular.

Nouns ending in **s, ß, x, z, tz** always add **–es**. The genitive of place names ending in an **–s** is avoided: **die Strassen von Paris** *the streets of Paris.*

Feminine nouns have no declensional endings, except that proper names add **–s** in the genitive: **Maries Mutter,** *Mary's mother.*

Some masculine nouns add **–n** or **–en** for all cases except the nominative:

N.	der Student	der Junge	der Herr
G.	des Studenten	des Jungen	des Herrn
D.	dem Studenten	dem Jungen	dem Herrn
A.	den Studenten	den Jungen	den Herrn

A few masculine nouns and **das Herz** have unexpected variations:

N.	der Name	das Herz
G.	des Namens	des Herzens
D.	dem Namen	dem Herzen
A.	den Namen	das Herz

The following nouns are declined like **der Name:**

der Friede, des Friedens, etc.
der Gedanke, des Gedankens, etc.
der Glaube, des Glaubens, etc.
der Wille, des Willens, etc.

2) Declension of Nouns with **ein**-words

The **ein-**words are **ein, kein** and the possessive adjectives.

mein	my	**unser**	our
dein	your	**euer**	your
sein	his, its	**ihr**	their
ihr	her, its	**Ihr**	your
sein	its		

The endings on the **ein-**words vary from those of the **der-**words only in the masculine nominative and the neuter nominative and accusative, where the **ein-**words have no endings.

	M.	F.	N.
N.	*ein* Tisch	meine Uhr	*unser* Zimmer
G.	eines Tisches	meiner Uhr	unseres Zimmers
D.	einem Tisch(e)	meiner Uhr	unserem Zimmer
A.	einen Tisch	meine Uhr	*unser* Zimmer

Certain forms of **unser** and **euer** are commonly contracted: **uns(e)re, uns(e)res, unser(e)m, unser(e)n, uns(e)rer.**

3) Nominative Case

The nominative case designates subjects, predicate nouns (subjective complements), and nouns of address.

Wo ist Ihr Zimmer?	Where is your room?
Jener Herr ist mein Onkel.	That man is my uncle.
Mein Freund, was hast du in der Hand?	My friend, what do you have in your hand?

The indefinite article is not used with a predicate noun denoting profession, nationality, or religion, unless an attributive adjective is present.

Er ist Arzt.	He is a physician.
Ich bin Amerikaner.	I am an American.
Ist er Muselman?	Is he a Moslem?
Er ist ein berühmter Arzt.	He is a famous physician.

4) Genitive Case

The genitive case expresses possession, description, and indefinite time.

Das ist das Haus meines Vaters.	That is my father's house.
Ein Mann hohen Alters geht jeden Tag in die Bibliothek.	A man of advanced age goes to the library every day.
Er ist derselben Meinung.	He is of the same opinion.
Eines Tages besuchten wir das Schloß.	One day we visited the castle.

The genitive forms **morgens, vormittags, mittags, nachmittags, abends,** and **nachts** have become adverbs and are not capitalized.

Er macht morgens (abends, nachts) einen Spaziergang.	He takes a walk mornings (in the morning, evenings, in the evening, at night).

Certain prepositions and certain verbs require genitive objects.*

* Prepositions are presented in Lesson 5, and verbs with genitive and dative objects in Lesson 12.

5) Dative Case

The dative case designates the indirect object with transitive verbs of giving, taking, telling, and showing. The indirect object precedes the direct object unless the direct object is a pronoun.

Wir geben dem Mann ein Buch.	We are giving the man a book.
Wir geben ihm ein Buch.	We are giving him a book.
Wir geben es dem Mann.	We are giving it to the man.
Wir geben es ihm.	We are giving it to him.
Jemand nimmt dem Mann das Buch.	Somebody is taking the book from the man.

Dative forms are used idiomatically in place of possessive adjectives or the genitive case in association with articles of clothing and parts of the body.

Der Junge tritt seiner Schwester auf den Fuß.	The boy steps on his sister's foot.
Er tritt ihr auf den Fuß.	He steps on her foot.

Certain prepositions and certain verbs require dative objects.

6) Accusative Case

The accusative case is used for the direct object of transitive verbs, definite time, duration of time, measure of distance, and the absolute construction.

Sie schreibt einen Brief.	She is writing a letter.
Er geht jeden Tag in die Stadt.	He goes to town every day.
Wir studieren den ganzen Tag.	We study all day.
Wer läuft jeden Tag eine Meile?	Who runs a mile every day?
Den Hut in der Hand, sitze ich in der Sonne.	My hat in my hand, I sit in the sun.

A few verbs can have two accusative objects:

fragen	ask	**rufen**	call
heißen	call	**schelten**	call (an uncomplimentary name)
kosten	cost	**schimpfen**	call (an uncomplimentary name)
lehren	teach	**taufen**	baptize
nennen	name, call		

Er nennt (heißt, schilt, schimpft) mich einen Dummkopf.	He calls me a blockhead.
Das Mittagessen kostet jedes Mädchen einen Dollar.	Lunch costs each girl a dollar.
Er fragte mich den Namen des Kindes.	He asked me the child's name.

Certain prepositions require the accusative case.

7) The definite article is used with nouns expressing abstract or generalized meanings, with the names of days, months, and seasons, and with names of countries having the article **die**.

Die jungen Leute sind immer froh.	Young people are always happy.
Die Philosophen sprechen oft von der Wahrheit und der Schönheit.	Philosophers often talk about truth and beauty.
Am Montag ist die Schule aus.	On Monday school will be out.
Im Juli ist es immer heiß.	In July it is always hot.
Im Frühling fährt er gerne aufs Land.	In the spring he likes to drive to the country.
Nächste Woche fliegen wir in die Schweiz.	Next week we are flying to Switzerland.

8) The use of the definite and indefinite articles varies somewhat between German and English. Note the following distinctions.

Gehen Sie zweimal *die* Woche (in *der* Woche) ins Kino?	Do you go to the movies twice *a* week?
Das Fleisch kostet vier Mark *das* Pfund.	The meat costs four marks *a* pound.

9) The definite article replaces the possessive adjective if there is no ambiguity.

Er hat die Hand in der Tasche.	He has his hand in his pocket.

10) The names of places and of months stand in apposition to the nouns **Stadt, Monat,** etc. Also, nouns representing quantity and material stand in apposition to each other.

die Stadt Hamburg	the city of Hamburg
das Land Italien	the land of Italy
im Monat Juli	in the month of July
eine Tasse Kaffee	a cup of coffee
diese Art Brot	this kind of bread
eine Menge Leute	a crowd of people

11) Word Order

The inflected verb stands in second position in a main clause. The subject may stand first or third. Any element of the predicate may occupy the first position for emphasis.

Er geht jeden Tag in die Stadt.	He goes to town every day.
Jeden Tag geht er in die Stadt.	Every day he goes to town.
In die Stadt geht er jeden Tag.	He goes to town every day.

In questions containing interrogative elements the interrogative word or phrase stands first, with the verb immediately following. The subject is either first or third.

Wer geht jeden Tag in die Stadt?	Who goes to town every day?
In welche Stadt geht er jeden Tag?	To which town does he go every day?

In questions not containing interrogative elements, the verb stands first and the subject second.

Geht er jeden Tag in die Stadt?	Does he go to town every day?

ORAL EXERCISES

A. Verb Stems plus −er

The ending **−er** attached to a verb stem produces a masculine noun representing the person or instrument performing the action of the verb. The stem vowel is frequently umlauted.

Examples: **der Käufer** purchaser; **der Sprecher** speaker; **der Wecker** alarm clock

The feminine equivalent for persons is obtained by adding **-in** to the **-er**: **die Sprecherin** (feminine) speaker; **die Käuferin** (feminine) purchaser.

B. *Study the following verbs and their noun derivatives. Note that the stem vowel sometimes is umlauted.*

halten	to hold	**der Halter**	holder, reservoir
kaufen	to buy	**der Käufer**	buyer, purchaser
schlagen	to hit	**der Schläger**	brawler, tennis racket, golf club
		der Schlager	(popular) hit (*song, play, book*)
wecken	to waken	**der Wecker**	alarm clock
zeigen	to show	**der Zeiger**	pointer, needle, hand (*of clock*)

C. *Name the verbs from which the following nouns are derived.*

der Bäcker	baker	**der Räuber**	robber
der Empfänger	recipient	**der Schläfer**	sleeper
der Flieger	flyer	**der Spieler**	player, actor, gambler
der Führer	leader, guide	**der Tänzer**	dancer
der Läufer	runner	**die Tänzerin**	dancer
die Läuferin	runner	**der Zauberer**	magician, juggler
der Löscher	extinguisher, blotter		

WRITTEN EXERCISE

1. The man gave this boy his watch.
2. He became a famous runner last year.
3. Who stepped on the girl's hand?
4. He is buying his friend's wife a glass of wine.
5. Her sister studied German all evening.
6. One morning we had a test.
7. She asks each child his name.
8. Which poet wrote about love and war?

9. She will become a salesgirl next month.
10. Every day we sent them to him.
11. His dog on a leash, the boy walked through the park.
12. A crowd of happy people attended the party.
13. Mr. Meier, which student is your son?
14. His song was a hit last year.
15. The teacher often forgot his servant's name.
16. He put his money into his pocket.
17. Sundays we take a walk into the country.
18. I took the letter from the gentleman.
19. Are you of this opinion too?
20. Our neighbor is the baker here.

LESSON 2

SIMPLE TENSE FORMS, INDICATIVE

---

12) Weak and Strong Verbs

There are two general categories of verbs: weak and strong. Weak verbs are recognized by their lack of vowel change and by the presence of **t** in the simple past form and the perfect (*or* past) participle.

Example: **machen, machte, gemacht**

Strong verbs are recognized by at least one vowel change in the principal parts. The present and simple past indicative forms always have different vowels. The perfect participle ends in **–en.**

Example: **schreiben, schrieb, geschrieben**

13) Present Indicative of Weak Verbs

To the stem of the verb, obtained by removing **–en** or **–n** from the infinitive, the personal endings **–e, –st, –t, –en, –t, –en** are added to form the present tense. When the combination of the stem and the prescribed ending is unpronounceable, the vowel **–e** is inserted. This often happens with stems ending in **d, t, m,** or **n.** The **s** of the second singular ending is not added when the stem ends in a sibilant (**s, ß, tz, zz**). For verbs of this type, the second and third singular are pronounced and spelled alike.

machen	reden	reisen	öffnen	lächeln
to make, do	to speak	to travel	to open	to smile
ich mache	ich rede	ich reise	ich öffne	ich lächele
du machst	du redest	du reist	du öffnest	du lächelst
er macht	er redet	er reist	er öffnet	er lächelt
wir machen	wir reden	wir reisen	wir öffnen	wir lächeln
ihr macht	ihr redet	ihr reist	ihr öffnet	ihr lächelt
sie machen	sie reden	sie reisen	sie öffnen	sie lächeln
Sie machen	Sie reden	Sie reisen	Sie öffnen	Sie lächeln

The first and third plural and the formal second person have the same form as the infinitive. The only exception is the irregular **sein: wir sind, sie sind, Sie sind.**

14) Past Indicative of Weak Verbs

To the stem of the verb is added the tense ending **t** with the personal endings **–e, –est, –e, –en, –et, –en.** When the combination of the stem and the tense ending **t** is unpronounceable, the vowel **e** is inserted between them.

machen	reden	reisen	öffnen	lernen
to make, do	to speak	to travel	to open	to learn
ich machte	ich redete	ich reiste	ich öffnete	ich lernte
du machtest	du redetest	du reistest	du öffnetest	du lerntest
er machte	er redete	er reiste	er öffnete	er lernte
wir machten	wir redeten	wir reisten	wir öffneten	wir lernten
ihr machtet	ihr redetet	ihr reistet	ihr öffnetet	ihr lerntet
sie machten	sie redeten	sie reisten	sie öffneten	sie lernten
Sie machten	Sie redeten	Sie reisten	Sie öffneten	Sie lernten

15) Present Indicative of Strong Verbs

Many strong verbs form their present tense in the same manner as weak verbs. Some strong verbs have a change of vowel in the second and third singular. This change may be an umlauted stem vowel or a change of **e** to **ie** or **i**. Verbs with stems ending in sibilants have the same sound and spelling in the second and third singular.

gehen	sehen	sprechen	halten	sitzen
to go	to see	to speak	to hold	to sit
ich gehe	ich sehe	ich spreche	ich halte	ich sitze
du gehst	du siehst	du sprichst	du hältst	du sitzt
er geht	er sieht	er spricht	er hält*	er sitzt
wir gehen	wir sehen	wir sprechen	wir halten	wir sitzen
ihr geht	ihr seht	ihr sprecht	ihr haltet	ihr sitzt
sie gehen	sie sehen	sie sprechen	sie halten	sie sitzen
Sie gehen	Sie sehen	Sie sprechen	Sie halten	Sie sitzen

16) Past Indicative of Strong Verbs

The past indicative stems must be learned individually. Most strong verbs belong to one of seven classes (see appendix, page 133). The first and third person singular have no personal endings. The remaining forms have the same endings as those of the present tense. An **e** may be needed before the second person ending when the past stem ends in **d** or **t**. Past stems ending in a sibilant require **–est** in the second singular.

gehen	sehen	sprechen	halten	sitzen
to go	to see	to speak	to hold	to sit
ich ging	ich sah	ich sprach	ich hielt	ich saß
du gingst	du sahst	du sprachst	du hieltest	du saßest
er ging	er sah	er sprach	er hielt	er saß
wir gingen	wir sahen	wir sprachen	wir hielten	wir saßen
ihr gingt	ihr saht	ihr spracht	ihr hieltet	ihr saßt
sie gingen	sie sahen	sie sprachen	sie hielten	sie saßen
Sie gingen	Sie sahen	Sie sprachen	Sie hielten	Sie saßen

* A few verbs which have a stem ending in **d** or **t** assimilate the **–t** ending into the stem: **er brät** (**braten** *to roast*); **er lädt** (**laden** *to load*); **er rät** (**raten** *to advise*); **er schilt** (**schelten** *to scold*) **er tritt** (**treten** *to step*).

17) Modal Auxiliaries and **wissen**

The principal parts of the modal auxiliaries and **wissen** are:

dürfen	**darf**	**durfte**	**gedurft**	to be allowed to
können	**kann**	**konnte**	**gekonnt**	to be able to
mögen	**mag**	**mochte**	**gemocht**	to like to
müssen	**muß**	**mußte**	**gemußt**	to have to
sollen	**soll**	**sollte**	**gesollt**	to be supposed to
wollen	**will**	**wollte**	**gewollt**	to want to
wissen	**weiß**	**wußte**	**gewußt**	to know (*factual information*)

können		**wissen**	
PRESENT	PAST	PRESENT	PAST
ich kann	**ich konnte**	**ich weiß**	**ich wußte**
du kannst	**du konntest**	**du weißt**	**du wußtest**
er kann	**er konnte**	**er weiß**	**er wußte**
wir können	**wir konnten**	**wir wissen**	**wir wußten**
ihr könnt	**ihr konntet**	**ihr wißt**	**ihr wußtet**
sie können	**sie konnten**	**sie wissen**	**sie wußten**
Sie können	**Sie konnten**	**Sie wissen**	**Sie wußten**

18) Weak Verbs with Vowel Change in their Principal Parts

A limited number of verbs form their principal parts with a **t** typical of weak verbs, but also with a different vowel in the past indicative and in the perfect participle. *Example:* **kennen, kannte, gekannt.**

kennen to know (be acquainted with)		**bringen** to bring	
PRESENT	PAST	PRESENT	PAST
ich kenne	**ich kannte**	**ich bringe**	**ich brachte**
du kennst	**du kanntest**	**du bringst**	**du brachtest**
er kennt	**er kannte**	**er bringt**	**er brachte**
wir kennen	**wir kannten**	**wir bringen**	**wir brachten**
ihr kennt	**ihr kanntet**	**ihr bringt**	**ihr brachtet**
sie kennen	**sie kannten**	**sie bringen**	**sie brachten**
Sie kennen	**Sie kannten**	**Sie bringen**	**Sie brachten**

denken to think

PRESENT	PAST
ich denke	ich dachte
du denkst	du dachtest
er denkt	er dachte
wir denken	wir dachten
ihr denkt	ihr dachtet
sie denken	sie dachten
Sie denken	Sie dachten

Other verbs conjugated like **kennen** are **brennen** *to burn,* **nennen** *to call,* **rennen** *to run,* **senden** *to send,* and **wenden** *to turn.*

19) Imperative Forms

German verbs have three imperative forms. The singular familiar imperative generally consists of the stem with the ending **-e:**

Gehe! Go. **Arbeite!** Work.

However, verbs with a vowel change to **ie** or **i** retain the change in the singular imperative form and do not add **-e:**

Sieh! Look. **Sprich!** Speak.

The plural familiar imperative is identical with the second plural form of the present tense, but the subject pronoun is not used:

Geht! Go. **Arbeitet!** Work. **Seht!** Look. **Sprecht!** Speak.

The formal imperative is stated by reversing the subject and verb of the formal address:

Gehen Sie! Go. **Arbeiten Sie!** Work. **Sehen Sie!** Look.

The exclamation point is always used with imperative forms in German.

20) Three verbs are so irregular that they must be learned separately.

sein to be   **haben** to have

PRESENT	PAST	PRESENT	PAST
ich bin	ich war	ich habe	ich hatte
du bist	du warst	du hast	du hattest
er ist	er war	er hat	er hatte
wir sind	wir waren	wir haben	wir hatten
ihr seid	ihr wart	ihr habt	ihr hattet
sie sind	sie waren	sie haben	sie hatten
Sie sind	Sie waren	Sie haben	Sie hatten

werden to become

PRESENT	PAST
ich werde	ich wurde
du wirst	du wurdest
er wird	er wurde
wir werden	wir wurden
ihr werdet	ihr wurdet
sie werden	sie wurden
Sie werden	Sie wurden *

IMPERATIVES

sei!	habe!	werde!
seid!	habt!	werdet!
seien Sie!	haben Sie!	werden Sie!

21) Uses of the Present Indicative

German has only one present indicative tense, whereas English has three variations.

Er schläft.   He sleeps (he is sleeping, he does sleep).

* The formal address forms are not listed in subsequent conjugation patterns.

As in English, the present tense frequently refers to future time, especially when the context contains a clear reference to the future.

Er studiert nächstes Jahr Deutsch.   He is studying (will study, is going to study) German next year.

The present tense also describes a condition or action that has begun in the past and is still in effect. Frequently **schon** and/or **seit** accompanies this meaning.

Ich wohne schon drei Jahre hier.
Ich wohne seit drei Jahren hier.   I have been living here for three years.

Er arbeitet seit einem Jahre in einer Fabrik.
Er arbeitet schon seit einem Jahre in einer Fabrik.   He has been working in a factory for a year.

22) Uses of the Simple Past Indicative

German has only one simple past form.

Er schlief am Tage.   He slept (he was sleeping, he did sleep, he used to sleep) in the daytime.

The simple past form usually implies progressive action, description, or repetition.*

Er sprach mit dem Professor.   He was talking to the professor.
Die Sonne schien.   The sun shone (was shining).
Die Vögel sangen.   The birds sang (were singing).
Ich aß jeden Tag in einem Restaurant.   I ate (used to eat) in a restaurant every day.

The simple past tense, frequently with **schon** or **seit,** describes a condition or action beginning in the past and continuing up to a point of time in the past.

Er arbeitete schon zwei Jahre in einer Fabrik.   He had been working in a factory for two years (and was still working there).

---

* Single completed actions are expressed in the present perfect tense:
Was haben Sie gekauft? What did you buy? *or* What have you bought? *but not* What were you buying?

23) Infinitives without **zu**

The modal auxiliaries take a complementary infinitive without **zu**. The modal auxiliary occupies the customary second position in a main clause and the complementary infinitive stands last.

Man kann jeden Tag etwas lernen.   You can learn something every day.

Other verbs that take complementary infinitives without **zu** are

fühlen	to feel	**lassen**	to permit, cause
haben	to have	**lehren**	to teach
heißen	to order	**lernen**	to learn
helfen	to help	**sehen**	to see
hören	to hear		

In gewissen Orten fühlt man die Erde beben.   In certain places you feel the earth tremble.

Die Frau läßt ihren Sohn ein Auto kaufen.   The woman is letting her son buy a car.

Sie läßt ihrer Tochter ein Kleid machen.   She is having a dress made for her daughter.

Wer hat den Text vor sich liegen?   Who has the text (lying) in front of him?

24) Infinitives with **zu**

Infinitives following verbs other than those named above use **zu**. Note especially that **wissen** requires **zu**.

Der Professor weiß (versteht), die Klasse zu unterhalten.   The professor knows how to entertain the class.

ORAL EXERCISES

A. Many nouns are derived from verbs. *Compare the meanings of the following nouns derived from the verb* **binden** *to tie or bind.*

der **Band**	volume (book)	die **Binde**	bandage, string
das Band	ribbon, tie, bond	**der Bund**	band, alliance
die Bande	troop, gang	**das Bund**	bundle, bunch
			(*of keys*)

B. Some noun derivatives consist of the verb stem. Their gender is unpredictable. *Name the verbs related to the following nouns.*

der Anfang	beginning	**der Preis**	price, prize,
der Bau	building		reward
der Befehl	command	**der Rat**	advice, assembly
der Bericht	report		(for delibera-
der Beruf	calling, vocation,		tion)
	profession	**der Raub**	robbery, prey,
der Besuch	visit, company		loot
	(visitors)	**der Ruf**	cry, summons,
der Betrag	amount, sum		reputation
	total	**der Schein**	light (*of sun,*
der Beweis	proof,		*etc.*), appear-
	demonstration		ance, illusion,
der Donner	thunder		certificate,
der Empfang	receipt (*of a letter*)		banknote
der Erfolg	success, result	**der Schlaf**	sleep
der Fall	fall, downfall,	**der Schlag**	blow, rap, stroke
	case	**der Schmerz**	pain, grief
der Fluch	curse, oath	**der Schreck**	terror
der Gewinn	gain, profit	**der Schrei**	scream, cry
der Lauf	course, path,	**der Sinn**	sense, mind,
	progress		meaning

der Sitz	seat, residence	**die Antwort**	answer
der Spalt	crack, crevice, slit	**die Arbeit**	work, labor, employment
der Steig	footpath	**die Dauer**	duration, constancy
der Stoß	push, nudge, impact	**die Gestalt**	form, shape, stature
der Streich	stroke, trick, prank	**die Last**	load, burden, cargo
der Verfall	decay, decline, decadence	**die Schau**	show, exhibition
der Vergleich	comparison, compromise	**die Tracht**	dress, costume
der Verkehr	traffic, commerce, trade	**das Bad**	bath, health resort (*with water*)
der Verstoß	offense, mistake, blunder	**das Grab**	grave
der Versuch	attempt, experiment	**das Kleid**	garment, dress (*pl.* clothes)
der Vertrag	agreement, treaty	**das Leid**	sorrow, hurt, wrong
der Verweis	reprimand, rebuke	**das Spiel**	game, play, performance
der Wink	sign, nod, hint	**das Urteil**	decision, judgment, sentence
der Würfel	cube, die (*pl.* dice)	**das Verhör**	trial, hearing
die Acht	attention		

C. Nouns formed by adding **–e** to the verb stem are feminine. *Name the verbs related to the following nouns.*

die Binde	bandage, string	**die Reise**	journey, trip
die Bitte	request	**die Sage**	saying, legend,
die Falle	trap		saga
die Fliege	fly	**die Schere**	scissors
die Frage	question	**die Schließe**	pin, bolt,
die Habe	possessions		fastener
die Hebe	lever, pulley	**die Schlinge**	noose, loop,
die Lehre	doctrine, theory,		snare
	precept	**die Schmelze**	melting, fusion
die Lese	collecting,	**die Schneide**	knife edge, cut
	harvest	**die Schraube**	screw
die Liebe	love	**die Spalte**	slit, crack, col-
die Lüge	lie		umn of print
die Mühe	trouble, toil	**die Spinne**	spider
die Pflanze	plant	**die Stelle**	place
die Pflege	care, rearing,	**die Trage**	litter, stretcher
	nursing	**die Wiege**	cradle
die Quelle	spring, well,		
	source		

D. Some nouns sound like the past forms of strong verbs. Except for **die Tat,** the feminine derivatives add an **–e**. *Name the related verbs.*

der Band	volume (*book*)	**der Griff**	handhold, knob,
der Biß	bite, sting		handle
der Drang	crowd, urgency,	**der Klang**	sound, ringing
	pressure		(*of bells*),
der Fraß	food (*for animals*)		timbre
		der Pfiff	whistle, trifle

der Riß	tear, gap, crack		
der Ritt	ride (*on horse-back*)	**die Tat**	deed, act, action
		die Aufnahme	absorption, admission, photograph
der Schmiß	blow, cut, dueling scar		
der Schnitt	cut, incision	**die Ausnahme**	exception
der Schritt	step, stride, pace	**die Bande**	troop, band
der Schwamm	sponge	**die Gabe**	present, offering, talent
der Stand	condition, class, rank		
		die Grube	mine, hole, ditch
der Strich	line, stripe		
der Trank	drink, beverage	**die Lage**	situation, position, site
der Trieb	impetus, impulse, instinct		
		die Schlange	snake
		die Sprache	language
der Umstand	circumstance, condition	**die Stiege**	staircase, flight of stairs
der Unterschied	distinction, difference	**das Band**	ribbon, tie, bond
der Verband	joint, bandage, union	**das Floß**	raft
		das Gebot	command
der Verstand	understanding, intellect, intelligence	**das Maß**	measure
		das Schloß	lock, castle
		das Verbot	prohibition
der Wuchs	growth, figure, height		

WRITTEN EXERCISE

1. We (will) now write some sentences.
2. The students must write them on the blackboard.
3. One finds the beginning easy; the answer is (stands) always in the book.
4. Sometimes I ask for advice and the teacher advises me.
5. Then I know (how) to complete my work.
6. "Last week you were reading a story about Wilhelm Tell," said the teacher.
7. We were also speaking about the legend of Tell.
8. You opened your book and saw his son.
9. The boy was standing under a tree; he was not wearing a hat.
10. The father gives the boy an apple, but he is not allowed to eat it.
11. Since that day he has not liked apples at all.
12. Were you visiting your uncle in the month of July?
13. My brother and I visited him on the Fourth of July.
14. We looked for his house and could not find it.
15. He had lived in that house for only a few months.
16. We were driving too fast and there was too much traffic.
17. We had to find a well and a footpath.
18. We were supposed to arrive earlier, but we could not do it.
19. Our friends were studying their lessons; they were not sleeping.
20. Did you know that you are not allowed to smoke here?

LESSON 3

25) Personal Pronouns

Personal pronouns replace nouns and agree with those nouns in gender and number. The genitive forms of the personal pronouns are rare in modern German, usually appearing with verbs that take genitive complements.*

N.	ich	du	er	sie	es	wir	ihr	sie	Sie
G.	meiner	deiner	seiner	ihrer	seiner	unser	euer	ihrer	Ihrer
D.	mir	dir	ihm	ihr	ihm	uns	euch	ihnen	Ihnen
A.	mich	dich	ihn	sie	es	uns	euch	sie	Sie

Wo ist mein Hut? Ich kann ihn nicht finden.	Where is my hat? I can't find it.
Ich gehe in die Klasse. Sie beginnt um zehn Uhr.	I am going to class. It begins at ten o'clock.
Ich erinnere mich seiner gut.*	I remember him well.

Modern usage permits **sie** for **das Mädchen** and **das Fräulein.**

Ich kenne das Mädchen nicht. Kennst du sie?	I don't know the girl. Do you know her?

* Verbs with genitive complements are discussed in Lesson 12.

The German equivalent of *It is I* (*me*) uses the subject pronoun with the corresponding verb form.

Ich bin es.	It is I (me).	**Wir sind es.**	It is we (us).
Du bist es.	It is you.	**Ihr seid es.**	It is you.
Er ist es.	It is he (him).	**Sie sind es.**	It is they (them).
		Sie sind es.	It is you.

Personal pronouns that do not refer to people or animals are replaced by **da–** in combination with prepositions governing the dative or accusative case, just as in English *therewith, thereto,* etc. are occasionally used. An **r** is inserted if the preposition begins with a vowel.

Hier ist ein Kästchen. Was ist darin?	Here is a little box. What is in it (therein)?

Exceptions: **außer, bis, ohne** and **seit** are never combined with **da** or **wo.**

Wo ist mein Bleistift? Ohne ihn kann ich nicht schreiben.	Where is my pencil? Without it I can't write.

26) Impersonal **es**

Es is also used impersonally; i.e., not replacing a previously mentioned noun. It may stand for nothing at all, as in statements about weather, or it may anticipate a noun or a syntactical unit functioning as a noun in the context.

Es gibt einen Gott.	There is a God.
Es ist noch ein Student in der Klasse.	There is one more student in the class.
Es sind mehr Studenten heute in der Klasse.	There are more students in the class today.
Es regnet heute.	It is raining today.
Es ist wahr, daß wir fleißig studieren müssen.	It is true that we must study hard.

(**Es** merely anticipates the clause beginning with **daß.** The **daß**-clause is the true subject, as indicated by asking the question **Was ist wahr?**)

27) Demonstrative das and dies

Das and **dies** are demonstrative pronouns used much like **es**, but they give more emphasis than **es**.

Das weiß ich nicht.⎫
Ich weiß es nicht. ⎭   I don't know (that).

Das (dies) sind meine Bücher.   They (those, these) are my books.

28) Interrogative Pronouns

The interrogative pronouns **wer** and **was** refer to people and things, respectively.

N.	**wer**	**was**
G.	**wessen**	—
D.	**wem**	—
A.	**wen**	**was**

Wer ist das?   Who is that?

Was ist das?   What is that?

Wessen Auto steht vor der Tür?   Whose car is in front of the door?

Wem geben Sie dieses Bild?   To whom are you giving this picture?

Wen sehen Sie da?   Whom do you see there?

Was is avoided with prepositions by combining the preposition with **wo–** or **wor–**.

Womit malen Sie? Ich male mit Wasserfarben.   What do you paint with? I paint with water colors.

Sometimes the interrogative adjective **welcher, welche, welches** serves as a pronoun. The form is neuter unless a specific noun is implied.

Welcher hat das Glas zerbrochen?   Who (which boy) broke the glass?

Welches ist der jüngste Sohn?   Which one is the youngest son?

Welches ist der längste Fluß in Europa?   Which (what) is the longest river in Europe?

In the phrase **was für (ein)**, meaning *what kind of*, **für** does not function as a preposition. **Was** and **für** may be separated by other words.

Was für ein Hund ist das?   What kind of dog is that?

Was sind das für Bücher?   What kind of books are these (those)?

29) Demonstrative Pronouns

Demonstrative pronoun forms resembling those of the definite article can be used in place of the personal pronouns of the third person when special emphasis is required.

	M.	F.	N.	PL.
N.	der	die	das	die
G.	dessen	deren	dessen	deren
D.	dem	der	dem	denen
A.	den	die	das	die

Derjenige (*that, that one*) and **derselbe** (*the same*) are declined as follows:

	M.	F.	N.	PL.
N.	derjenige	diejenige	dasjenige	diejenigen
G.	desjenigen	derjenigen	desjenigen	derjenigen
D.	demjenigen	derjenigen	demjenigen	denjenigen
A.	denjenigen	diejenige	dasjenige	diejenigen

Kennen Sie den?	Do you know him (that man)?
Ja, der wohnt nicht weit von mir.	Yes, he lives not far from me.

The **der**-words and **ein**-words may also serve as demonstrative pronouns. The masculine nominative **ein** becomes **einer,** and the neuter nominative and accusative **ein** becomes **eines.**

Wessen Haus ist das? Es ist mein(e)s.	Whose house is that? It is mine.
Jeder weiß das.	Everybody knows that.
Nur einer hat das gesehen.	Only one (man) saw that.
Wir sehen zwei Männer. Keiner liest die Zeitung.	We see two men. Neither is reading the paper.

Dieser and **jener** have the same relation to each other as do *the latter* and *the former*.

Meine Mutter und meine Schwester spielen Klavier. Diese liebt Beethoven, jene liebt Gershwin.	My mother and my sister play the piano. The latter likes Beethoven; the former likes Gershwin.

30) Indefinite Pronouns

The indefinite **man** is extremely common in German, often serving to avoid a passive verb form.

Man kann von hier aus die ganze Stadt sehen.	You (we, a person) can see the whole city from here. (The whole city can be seen from here.)
Man öffnet die Bibliothek um sieben Uhr.	The library opens (is opened) at seven o'clock.

Other indefinite pronouns are **jemand** *somebody*, **niemand** *nobody*, and **jedermann** *everybody*.

N.	man	jemand	niemand	jedermann
G.	—	jemand(e)s	niemand(e)s	jedermanns
D.	einem	jemand(em)	niemand(em)	jedermann
A.	einen	jemand(en)	niemand(en)	jedermann

31) The Intensive Pronoun

Selbst or **selber** follows a noun or pronoun to give emphasis. **Selbst** as an adverb precedes what it modifies.

Ich selbst (selber) habe das gesehen. **Ich habe das selbst (selber) gesehen.**	I saw that myself.
Selbst ich kann das (tun).	Even I can do that.
Es kann selbst im Winter hier warm sein.	Even in the winter it can be warm here.

ORAL EXERCISE

Insert the correct German forms.

1. Ich sehe (*you, him, her, them*).

2. Siehst du (*me, us*)?

3. (*He*) bringt (*me, you, her, them*) einen Brief.

4. (*She*) erzählt (*me, us, him, them*) eine Geschichte (*herself*).

5. Ich brauche meine Feder (*myself*). Wo ist (*it*)?

6. Ich legte die Feder auf einen Tisch. Liegt (*it*) noch (*on it*)?

7. Alle Studenten sollen diese Aufgabe schreiben. (*It*) ist nicht lang.

8. (*Which*) ist die heutige Aufgabe? (*Even*) für (*you, them*) ist (*it*) leicht.

9. (*What*) ist (*that*)? (*It, that*) ist ein Elephant.

10. (*One, we, people*) findet dieses Tier interessant.

11. Wissen (*you*), ob (*it*) heute regnet?

12. (*Whom*) meinst du? Meinst du (*him, that man*)?

13. Es sind hier keine Stühle. (*On what*) sitzt (*one, a person*)?

14. (*Whose*) Hüte sind das? (*They*) gehören (*to them, to those people*).

15. Ich bringe meinen Bruder und seinen Freund mit. (*The latter*) singt und (*the former*) spielt Violine.

16. (*You*) kennst (*the former*), aber nicht (*the latter*).

17. (*Nobody*) weiß, (*what*) (*one*) (*about it*) tun soll.

18. Nur (*one*) kann den Preis gewinnen; nicht (*everybody*) kann es.

19. Ist (*that*) unser Lehrer? Nein, (*it is not he*).

20. (*It*) macht (*one, a person*) Freude, daß (*one*) etwas versteht.

WRITTEN EXERCISE

For friday

1. My dog is brown, and it has a short tail.

2. Tell me the answer yourself. It is easy.

3. Who will make the experiment? I will make it myself.

4. The figure in the picture is holding a certificate. Can you read it?

5. Sometimes there is not much rain here even in the month of April.

6. Do you think it will be nice tomorrow?

7. The wind was blowing hard; it whistled around the corner.

8. We remembered her for a long time.

9. The maid had lived in the house for many years, and now she had to leave it.

10. A book lay on the table, and in it was a flower.

11. I have a pencil and a pen; the latter has no ink, but you may use the former.

12. There are many kinds of animals in the world.

13. There are dogs, cats, and birds in the city.

14. Even that kind of tree does not grow in our state; it is too cold here.

15. Who knows something about the city of Dresden?

16. Ask Paul. His (*demonstrative pronoun*) parents lived in Dresden before the war.

17. In what are we supposed to mix the acid and the water?

18. You (one) always pour the former (*acid*) into the latter (*water*).

19. Then we will write the report. It will require one page.

20. Show this page to the teacher; he will read it right away.

LESSON 4

SIMPLE TENSE FORMS, SUBJUNCTIVE

32) Present Subjunctive Forms (Present I)

The present subjunctive forms of all verbs are obtained by adding the endings –e, –est, –e, –en, –et, –en to the stem.

machen to make, do   **sehen** to see

INDICATIVE	SUBJUNCTIVE	INDICATIVE	SUBJUNCTIVE
ich mache	ich mache	ich sehe	ich sehe
du machst	du machest	du siehst	du sehest
er macht	er mache	er sieht	er sehe
wir machen	wir machen	wir sehen	wir sehen
ihr macht	ihr machet	ihr seht	ihr sehet
sie machen	sie machen	sie sehen	sie sehen

dürfen   to be permitted to

INDICATIVE	SUBJUNCTIVE
ich darf	ich dürfe
du darfst	du dürfest
er darf	er dürfe
wir dürfen	wir dürfen
ihr dürft	ihr dürfet
sie dürfen	sie dürfen

29

Sein is irregular in the first and third singular; **haben** and **werden** take the regular endings.

INDICATIVE	SUBJUNCTIVE	INDICATIVE	SUBJUNCTIVE
ich bin	ich sei	ich habe	ich habe
du bist	du seiest	du hast	du habest
er ist	er sei	er hat	er habe
wir sind	wir seien	wir haben	wir haben
ihr seid	ihr seiet	ihr habt	ihr habet
sie sind	sie seien	sie haben	sie haben

INDICATIVE	SUBJUNCTIVE
ich werde	ich werde
du wirst	du werdest
er wird	er werde
wir werden	wir werden
ihr werdet	ihr werdet
sie werden	sie werden

33) Past Subjunctive Forms (Present II)

A. The past subjunctive forms of weak verbs are identical with their past indicative forms.

arbeiten to work

INDICATIVE	SUBJUNCTIVE
ich arbeitete	ich arbeitete
du arbeitetest	du arbeitetest
er arbeitete	er arbeitete
wir arbeiteten	wir arbeiteten
ihr arbeitetet	ihr arbeitetet
sie arbeiteten	sie arbeiteten

B. The past subjunctive forms of strong verbs are obtained by adding the endings **–e, –est, –e, –en, –et, –en** to the past indicative stem and by umlauting the stem vowel whenever possible.

gehen to go		**sitzen** to sit	
INDICATIVE	SUBJUNCTIVE	INDICATIVE	SUBJUNCTIVE
ich ging	ich ginge	ich saß	ich säße
du gingst	du gingest	du saßest	du säßest
er ging	er ginge	er saß	er säße
wir gingen	wir gingen	wir saßen	wir säßen
ihr gingt	ihr ginget	ihr saßt	ihr säßet
sie gingen	sie gingen	sie saßen	sie säßen

sehen to see	
INDICATIVE	SUBJUNCTIVE
ich sah	ich sähe
du sahst	du sähest
er sah	er sähe
wir sahen	wir sähen
ihr saht	ihr sähet
sie sahen	sie sähen

Strong verbs with stems ending in a consonant preceded by **l** or **r** may have a vowel not derived from that of the indicative past form.

helfen to help		**sterben** to die	
INDICATIVE	SUBJUNCTIVE	INDICATIVE	SUBJUNCTIVE
ich half	ich hülfe	ich starb	ich stürbe
du halfst	du hülfest	du starbst	du stürbest
er half	er hülfe	er starb	er stürbe
wir halfen	wir hülfen	wir starben	wir stürben
ihr halft	ihr hülfet	ihr starbt	ihr stürbet
sie halfen	sie hülfen	sie starben	sie stürben

For a few verbs, alternate forms have developed: **begönne** or **begänne** (from **beginnen**), **gewönne** or **gewänne** (from **gewinnen**), **schwömme** or **schwämme** (from **schwimmen**), **stünde** or **stände** (from **stehen**).

C. **Sein, haben** and **werden** have umlauted vowels.

INDICATIVE	SUBJUNCTIVE	INDICATIVE	SUBJUNCTIVE
ich war	ich wäre	ich hatte	ich hätte
du warst	du wärest	du hattest	du hättest
er war	er wäre	er hatte	er hätte
wir waren	wir wären	wir hatten	wir hätten
ihr wart	ihr wäret	ihr hattet	ihr hättet
sie waren	sie wären	sie hatten	sie hätten

INDICATIVE	SUBJUNCTIVE
ich wurde	ich würde
du wurdest	du würdest
er wurde	er würde
wir wurden	wir würden
ihr wurdet	ihr würdet
sie wurden	sie würden

D. The modal auxiliaries and the weak verbs with vowel change have the same vowel in the past subjunctive as in the infinitive. The exceptions are **wissen, bringen** and **denken,** which umlaut the vowel of the past indicative.

dürfen	er dürfte	he would be allowed to
können	er könnte	he would be able to, could
mögen	er möchte	he would like (to)
müssen	er müßte	he would have to
sollen	er sollte	he should, ought to
wollen	er wollte	he would want (to)
kennen	er kennte	he would know (recognize)

Exceptions:

wissen	er wüßte	he would know
bringen	er brächte	he would bring
denken	er dächte	he would think

34) Indirect Discourse with the Simple Verb Forms

There are three possible time relationships between the verb introducing the indirect discourse and the verb in the indirect discourse.

He said that he had no money. That is, he had no money at the time that he was saying so. Note that the English form *had* sounds like a past form, but that it merely indicates simultaneity with the making of the statement.

He said that he had had no money. That is, he had had no money at a time prior to making the statement. English uses a past perfect form to establish this prior relationship.

He said that he would have no money. That is, he anticipates having no money at a time subsequent to the action of saying so. English uses the auxiliary *would* to produce this effect.

The equivalent German statements have two choices of subjunctive forms. For the simultaneous effect, these two choices are the simple forms. As in English, the subordinating conjunction **daß** may be omitted. When it is omitted, the indirect discourse has normal word order.

Er sagte, daß er kein Geld habe.	
Er sagte, daß er kein Geld hätte.	He said (that) he had no money.
Er sagte, er habe (hätte) kein Geld.	

Both the present and the simple past subjunctive forms represent a relationship of simultaneity to the introductory verb. If one of these forms sounds like an indicative form, the other is necessarily used. If both forms sound like indicative forms, the second (or past) is always used.

Sie sagten, daß sie kein Geld hätten. (*not* **haben**)	They said that they had no money.
Sie sagten, daß sie ihre Aufgabe machten. (*not* **machen**)	They said that they were doing their lesson.

35) Indicative forms occur in indirect discourse under certain conditions.

A. When the introductory verb is in the first person.

Wir glauben, daß er recht hat.	We believe that he is right.

B. When legal and professional judgments are stated, unless the speaker means to disagree with the judgment.

Der Richter sagte, daß der Mann schuldig war.	The judge said that the man was guilty.
Der Arzt sagte, daß ich krank bin.	The doctor said that I am sick (and I accept his opinion).
Der Arzt sagte, daß ich krank sei (or wäre).	The doctor said that I was sick (but I don't agree with him).

C. In statements of generally accepted fact and statements following **wissen** or other words implying factual information.

Wir wissen, daß die Erde rund ist.	We know that the earth is round.
Es ist klar, daß er nicht alles versteht.	It is clear that he doesn't understand everything.
Die Tatsache, daß er etwas las, war ihm wichtig.	The fact that he was reading something was important to him.

36) Indirect Questions

The rules for choosing the verb form in indirect discourse apply also to indirect questions. **Ob** in indirect questions corresponds to the English *if* in the sense of *whether*.

Der Schaffner fragte mich, ob jemand neben mir sitze (säße).	The conductor asked me if (whether) somebody sat next to me.
Er fragte auch, wann ich ausstiege.	He also asked when I was getting off (would get off).
Er fragte, ob ich zum Speisewagen gehen wolle.	He asked whether I wanted to go to the dining car.
Er wartete, ob ich noch etwas wünschte.	He waited (to see) whether I wanted anything else.

37) Indirect Commands

In indirect commands a subjunctive form of **sollen** corresponds to the English *should*.

Der Lehrer sagte zu dem Jungen: "Mache das Buch zu!"	The teacher said to the boy, "Close the book."

Der Lehrer sagte, daß der Junge das Buch zumachen solle (sollte).	The teacher said that the boy should close the book.
Der Lehrer sagte, der Junge solle (sollte) das Buch zumachen.	The teacher said the boy should close the book.

38) Purpose Clauses with **damit** and **daß**

Purpose clauses following verbs in the present tense are stated with both indicative and subjunctive forms. The indicative form implies an assumption that the purpose will be accomplished.

Unser Freund arbeitet fleißig, damit seine Eltern auf ihn stolz sind.	Our friend works hard so that his parents will be proud of him.
Unser Freund arbeitet fleißig, damit seine Eltern auf ihn stolz seien.	Our friend works hard so that his parents may be (can be) proud of him.

39) Contrary-to-Fact Conditions in Present Time

Contrary-to-fact conditions (unreal conditions) are stated in both English and German with subjunctive verb forms. The following variations demonstrate the effect of the different verb forms in English.

If I have the money, I will go to Europe. Indicative forms show that the conclusion depends on another fact. The action referred to may or may not happen.

If I had the money, I would go to Europe. The subjunctive form *had*, which is a past form, refers to present time. It implies the negative of what is stated; i.e., *not* having money and *not* going to Europe.

If I had had the money, I would have gone to Europe. The past perfect subjunctive *had had* produces an unreal condition in past time.

In German, the contrary-to-fact condition uses the simple past subjunctive form in both clauses to refer to present time.* The condition (**wenn**-clause) is a subordinate clause, and the conclusion is the main clause.

* The **würde**-form is presented in Lesson 10.

Wenn ich das Geld hätte, führe ich nach Europa.	If I had the money, I would go to Europe.

If the conjunction **wenn** is not stated, the verb of the conditional clause stands first, as in English "*Had I the money . . .*"

Hätte ich das Geld, führe ich nach Europa.	Had I (if I had) the money, I would go to Europe.

Either clause may precede the other:

Ich führe nach Europa, wenn ich das Geld hätte.	I would go to Europe if I had the money.

When the **wenn-**clause stands first, **so** or **dann** is often found just before the verb of the conclusion.

Wenn wir mehr studierten, (so) könnten wir mehr verstehen.	If we studied more, (then) we could understand more.

40) Condition or Conclusion Standing Alone

Either clause of an unreal condition may stand alone. The condition represents a wish, often with the adverb **nur** or **doch**. The conclusion by itself indicates a theoretical proposition.

Wäre ich nur zu Hause!	If only I were at home!
Wenn ich nur singen könnte!	If I could only sing!
Wenn er doch endlich käme!	(I wish) that he would finally come.
Ich führe gerne nach Europa.	I would like to go to Europe.
Das könnte wahr sein.	That could be true.

41) Commands and Wishes with Present Subjunctive Forms

The present subjunctive form is inverted in the first person plural to indicate a general command.

Lesen wir weiter!	Let's read on.

The present subjunctive of third person forms may indicate a command or a wish.

Er komme herein!	Let (have) him come in.
Es lebe die Königin!	Long live the Queen!

42) als ob and als wenn

German expresses the equivalent of *as if* with **als ob** or **als wenn** and a subjunctive verb form. The omission of **ob** or **wenn** causes the verb to follow **als**.

Er sieht aus, als ob er krank sei (wäre).   He looks as if he were sick.

Er sieht aus, als sei (wäre) er krank.   He looks as if he were sick.

43) Subjunctive Forms to Show Respect

The past subjunctive forms of certain modal auxiliaries are used to show respect.

Dürfte ich Sie bitten, mir etwas zu erklären?   May (Might) I ask you to explain something to me?

Ich möchte Sie bitten, mir etwas zu erklären.   I would like to ask you to explain something to me.

ORAL EXERCISES

A. *Conjugate in the present and simple past subjunctive.*

1. haben	3. werden	5. verlieren
2. sein	4. dürfen	6. nehmen

B. *Give the subjunctive forms corresponding to the following indicative forms.*

1. ich weiß	6. er grub	11. sie essen	16. es brach
2. ich ging	7. wir bleiben	12. sie flogen	17. sie kann
3. du hast	8. wir fanden	13. Sie sind	18. es donnerte
4. du mußtest	9. ihr sollt	14. Sie kauften	19. wir warfen
5. er ist	10. ihr last	15. ich brachte	20. ihr schreibt

C. *Translate.*

1. He said he knew you.

2. That could not be true.

3. If I understood that, I would explain it to you.

4. If you had only been here!

5. Thy kingdom come!

6. If she only worked more!

7. May he become strong!

8. We would not be allowed to do that.

9. You told me you could swim.

10. Let's go to the movies.

WRITTEN EXERCISE

1. The teacher said this lesson was easy, but I say it is hard.

2. If I read the examples often enough, I would probably understand everything.

3. How could we travel in Germany if we didn't speak German?

4. Some people say that one doesn't have to speak the language of the country.

5. Did your neighbors believe that you had a new car?

6. Ask that man whether he works in this store.

7. He said that he was waiting for the salesman too.

8. If the salesman makes (lets) us wait long, I am going to a different store.

9. If he were helping us now, we could soon find what we want.

10. Let's look at that small picture; it would be a good choice for the dining room.

11. If a war started now, many of us would have to leave the university.

12. Some students act as if they had too much work.

13. If I knew that girl, I would tell (would name) you her name.

14. Let him speak! He would like to explain his theory.

15. It might rain today. Your mother said you should take an umbrella along.

16. If the king died, a prince would become king immediately.

17. The weather would be nice here if it were not so hot.

18. If only there were more rain in the summer!

19. The lawyer said that his client was not lying, but the judge said that somebody was lying.

20. I would like to read that book. May I borrow it from you?

LESSON 5

PREPOSITIONS

---

44) Certain prepositions always require accusative forms.

bis	**gegen**	**um**
durch	**ohne**	**wider**
für		

bis (up) to, until

Bis nächsten Donnerstag bleiben wir in der Stadt.	We are staying in town until next Thursday.
Zählen Sie von eins bis zwanzig.	Count from one to twenty.

Bis is usually followed by another preposition, which determines the case of the object:

Wir gingen bis zum Park.	We walked as far as the park.

durch through, by means of

Die Sonne scheint hell durch das Fenster.	The sun is shining brightly through the window.
Es kam durch die Post.	It came by mail.
Durch ihn habe ich die Stellung bekommen.	Through him (because of him) I got the job.

für for

Er hat 30 Mark für die Bücher bezahlt.	He paid 30 marks for the books.
Er dient für seinen Bruder.	He is serving for (in place of) his brother.
Diese Medizin ist gut für Sie.	This medicine is good for you.

gegen toward, against, in return for, in comparison with

Wir fahren gegen die Berge.	We are driving toward the mountains.
Die Armee kämpft gegen den Feind.	The army is fighting against the enemy.
Ich wette zehn gegen eins.	I'll bet ten to one.
Ein Schlager ist nichts gegen ein Kunstwerk.	A hit is nothing in comparison with a work of art.
Sie können Ihr Geld gegen eine Quittung bekommen.	You can get your money in return for a receipt.
Die Mutter ist immer gut gegen die Kinder.	The mother is always good to the children.
Haben Sie ein Heilmittel gegen Kopfschmerzen?	Do you have a medicine for (against) headaches?

ohne without

Ohne mich!	Count me out! (Without me!)
Heute essen wir ohne die Kinder.	Today we'll eat without the children.

um around, at (*time by clock*)

Die Erde kreist um die Sonne.	The earth orbits around the sun.
Um acht Uhr beginnt die Klasse.	The class begins at eight o'clock.
Um 1800 . . .	Around (the year) 1800 . . .
Sie sind um einen Kopf größer als ihr Vater.	They are a head taller (taller by a head) than their father.
Kaufen Sie dieses Bild um jeden Preis!	Buy this picture at any price (regardless of price)!

wider against (*only in the sense of resistance or opposition*)

Was hast du wider* mich (gegen mich)?	What do you have against me?

* **Wider** has disappeared from contemporary German, but it will be found in literature.

45) Certain prepositions always require dative forms.

aus	mit	von
außer	nach	zu
bei	seit	

aus out of, from, (made, composed) of

Ich komme aus dem Haus.	I am coming out of the house.
Wollen Sie ein Kleid aus Seide?	Do you want a dress (made) of silk?
Man sieht aus seinem Briefe, daß er glücklich ist.	You can tell (see) from his letter that he is happy.
Aus eigener Erfahrung weiß ich das.	I know that from my own experience.
Was ist aus ihm geworden?	What has become of him?
Viele Wissenschaftler kommen aus Ungarn.	Many scientists come from Hungary.

außer besides, except, but

Außer uns war niemand da.	Besides us nobody was there.

bei near, at the home (office) of, while (*doing something*), in (*weather*), by

Der Professor wohnte in Marbach bei Ludwigsburg.	The professor lived in Marbach near Ludwigsburg.
Ich wohne jetzt bei meinem Onkel.	I am living at my uncle's (house) now.
Beim Lesen kann man nicht auch noch Radio hören.	While reading you can't also listen to the radio.
Bei schlechtem Wetter fahren wir nicht.	We don't drive in bad weather.
Er nahm sie bei der Hand.	He took her by the hand.

mit with, by means of

Gehen Sie mit mir ins Theater?	Are you going to the theater with me?
Wir fahren mit dem Auto.	We are going by (means of the) car.
Man schlägt einen Nagel mit dem Hammer.	You hit a nail with the hammer.
Mit der Zeit wirst du es verstehen.	In time you will understand it.

nach after, toward, according to, to (*cities and countries*)

Nach dem Frühling kommt der Sommer.	After spring comes summer.
Wann fahren Sie nach Deutschland?	When are you going to Germany?
Nach meiner Meinung (meiner Meinung nach) ist er unschuldig.	In my opinion he is innocent.

seit since, for (*duration of time*)

Seit jenem Tag habe ich ihn nicht gesehen.	Since that day I have not seen him.
Seit einem Jahr reisen jene Leute durch Europa.	For a year those people have been traveling in Europe.

von by (*a person*), from, of (*to indicate possession or description*)

Der Junge wurde von seiner Mutter gerufen.	The boy was called by his mother.
Lesen Sie ein paar Gedichte von Schiller!	Read a few poems by Schiller.
Er kommt von Berlin.	He is coming from Berlin.
Das erste Semester läuft von September bis Januar.	The first semester lasts from September to January.
Das ist ein Freund von mir.	He (that) is a friend of mine.
Er ist ein Mann von Ehre.	He is a man of honor.

zu to, at

Gehen Sie geradeaus zum Bahnhof!	Go straight ahead to the railroad station.
Morgen muß ich zum Zahnarzt.	Tomorrow I have to go to the dentist.
Wir gehen auf dem Lande zu Fuß.	We walk (go on foot) in the country.
Wir haben sie zum letztenmal zu Weihnachten gesehen.	We saw them for the last time at Christmas.
Sie machten ihn zum Außenminister.	They made him Secretary of State.

46) Certain prepositions are accompanied by either dative or accusative forms.

an	**in**	**unter**
auf	**neben**	**vor**
hinter	**über**	**zwischen**

When these prepositions answer the question **wo** *at what place*, their objects are in the dative case. When they answer the question **wohin** *to what place*, their objects are in the accusative case.

Die Kinder laufen in das Haus.	The children run into the house.
Die Kinder laufen in dem Haus.	The children are running (around) in the house.
Ich saß zwischen der Tür und dem Fenster.	I was sitting between the door and the window.
Ich setzte mich zwischen die Tür und das Fenster.	I sat down (took a seat) between the door and the window.
Über dem Gebäude flattert die Fahne.	Above the building flies the flag.
Vögel fliegen über das Gebäude.	Birds fly over the building.

an to, on (*vertical surfaces*), at

Ein Bild hängt an der Wand.	A picture hangs on the wall.
Man hängt ein Bild an die Wand.	A picture is being hung on the wall.
Ein Professor liest an der Universität vor.	A professor lectures at the university.
Die Leiter lehnt an der Mauer.	The ladder is leaning on (against) the wall.
Gehe an das Fenster!	Go to the window.
Es ist an der Zeit.	The time is at hand. (It is time.)
Am Morgen sitzt der Dichter immer an seinem Schreibtisch.	In the morning the poet always sits at his desk.
Sind Sie noch an der Arbeit?	Are you still at work?
Alle tanzten bis an den Morgen.	Everybody danced until morning.
Der Wagen steht an der Ecke.	The car is at the corner.

auf on (*horizontal surfaces*), in, to

Die Katze klettert auf das Dach.	The cat climbs onto the roof.
Sie sitzt auf dem Dach.	It is sitting on the roof.

Studiert Ihr Sohn auf der Universität?	Is your son studying at the university?
Ich gehe auf mein Zimmer (die Post, die Bibliothek).	I am going to my room (the post office, the library).
Ich arbeite auf der Straße (dem Felde, dem Lande, dem Markt).	I work in the street (in the field, in the country, at the market).
Ostern fällt immer auf einen Sonntag.	Easter always comes (falls) on a Sunday.
Wir fahren auf einen Monat aufs Land.	We're going to the country for a month.

hinter behind

Hinter dem Hause steht ein Baum.	Behind the house is a tree.
Der Hund lief hinter das Haus.	The dog ran behind the house.
Was steckt hinter der Sache?	What's at the bottom of all this?

in in, into

Er fiel in den Teich.	He fell into the pool.
Er schwamm im Teich.	He was swimming in the pool.
In welcher Straße wohnen Sie?	On what street do you live?
Nur in der Nacht sieht man die Sterne.	You see the stars only at night.
Er blieb ihr treu bis in den Tod.	He remained faithful to her until death.

neben near, next to, beside(s)

Mein Hund geht immer neben mir.	My dog always walks beside me.
Der Sänger stellte sich neben das Klavier.	The singer took his place next to the piano.
Neben seinem Gehalt hat er andere Einkünfte.	He has other income besides (in addition to) his salary.

über over, above, about (concerning)

Ein Bild hängt über dem Sofa.	A picture hangs above the sofa.
Hängen Sie das Bild über das Sofa!	Hang the picture above the sofa.
Er wohnt über der Straße.	He lives across the street.

Wir fuhren über Frankfurt nach Basel.	We drove to Basel by way of Frankfurt.
Das geht über meinen Verstand.	That is beyond (goes over) my understanding.
Der König herrscht über sein Land.	The king rules (over) his country.
Heute über acht Tage sind wir da.	We'll be there a week from today.
Heute sprechen wir über einen neuen Roman.	Today we are talking about a new novel.

unter under, among

Der Hund kriecht unter den Stuhl.	The dog crawls under the chair.
Jetzt liegt er unter dem Stuhl.	Now he is lying under the chair.
Karl der Große brachte die Sachsen unter seine Herrschaft.	Charles the Great brought the Saxons under his rule.
Ich war unter den Zuschauern.	I was among the onlookers.
Was verstehen Sie unter dieser Idee?	What do you understand by (under) this idea?
Unter dieser Regierung hat man Freiheit.	Under this government you have freedom.

vor before, in front of, ago

Die Katze tritt vor den Kamin.	The cat steps up to (before) the fireplace.
Die Katze liegt vor dem Kamin.	The cat is lying in front of the fireplace.
Er flieht vor dem Feinde.	He runs before (from) the enemy.
Vor einem Jahr war es heißer.	A year ago it was hotter.
Er sprach vor sich hin.	He was talking to (in front of) himself.

zwischen between

Das Flugzeug fiel auf den freien Platz zwischen den Häusern.	The airplane fell on the open space between the houses.
Das Flugzeug fiel zwischen die Häuser.	The airplane fell between the houses.

47) Certain prepositions require genitive forms.

(an)statt	instead of	**diesseits**	on this side of
trotz	in spite of	**jenseits**	on the other side of
während	during	**außerhalb**	outside (of)
wegen	on account of	**innerhalb**	inside (of)
um . . . willen	for the sake of	**oberhalb**	above
		unterhalb	below

Trotz des Wetters spielt er Golf.	In spite of the weather he plays golf.
Wohnen Sie um Ihres Sohnes willen in der Stadt?	Do you live in the city for your son's sake?

48) Wegen and **willen** form compounds with the personal pronouns: **meinetwegen, deinetwegen, um ... seinetwillen,** etc.

Wohnen Sie um seinetwillen in der Stadt?	Do you live in the city for his sake?

49) Compounds with **wo-**

Wo- replaces an interrogative pronoun, just as **da-** replaces a personal pronoun, when the pronoun does not stand for a person. An **r** is inserted if the preposition begins with a vowel.

Womit schreiben Sie?	What are you writing with?
Worüber schreiben Sie?	What are you writing about?

50) Prepositions and definite articles are often contracted.

bei dem = beim	**durch das = durchs**
auf das = aufs	**in dem = im**

51) Anticipatory **da-** with Prepositions

When the impersonal **es** anticipates a clause and is the object of a preposition, it is replaced by **da-** or **dar-** combined with the preposition.

Erinnerst du dich daran, daß wir morgen eine Prüfung haben?	Do you remember (the fact) that we have a test tomorrow?
Er bestand darauf, im Büro zu rauchen.	He insisted on smoking in the office.

52) Prepositions with a daß-clause

Ohne and **anstatt** can take a **daß**-clause as an object.

Wir beobachteten ihn, ohne daß er uns bemerkte.	We watched him without his noticing us.
Er kam zu uns, anstatt daß wir zu ihm gingen.	He came to us instead of our going to him.

ORAL EXERCISES

A. Complete the German sentences.

Neben – beside
bei – near

1. Er kam (*through the forest*). *durch den Wald*
2. Sie geht (*without her hat*). *Ohne ihren hut*
3. Die Schule steht (*near the church*). *bei der Kirche*
4. Der Vogel sitzt (*in the nest*).
5. Er fuhr (*by train*). *mit dem Zug*
6. Sie warfen die Schuhe (*under the table*). *unter den Tisch*
7. Wir fuhren (*around the mountain*). *um den Berg*
8. Dieser Brief ist (*for him*). *für ihn*
9. (*During the class*) haben sie geschlafen. *Waren der Klasse*
10. Er sitzt (*behind his friend*).
11. (*Contrary to all expectation*) ist er gekommen. *gegen der Erwartung*
12. Ich sitze (*for an hour*) hier.
13. Sie haben (*an hour ago*) dagesessen.
14. Er kam (*without his books*) (*to school*).
15. Sind sie (*against me*) (*because of politics*)?
16. Der Mann setzt sich (*under the tree*). *unter dem Baum (den)*
17. Das Kind ist (*to him*) gelaufen. *zu ihm*
18. (*In spite of the weather*) gingen wir (*on foot*).
19. Der Stuhl steht (*next to the table*).
20. Der Junge lief (*between the houses*).

B. *Study the following choices of prepositions.*

in die Schule	to school (i.e., into the building)
nach Deutschland	to Germany (**nach** *with cities and countries*)
zum Frühstück (Mittagessen)	for breakfast (lunch)
zum Glück	luckily, fortunately
zu Hause	(at) home
nach Hause	home (*as destination*)

C. *Study the following expressions in which a preposition is used adverbially to modify the preceding prepositional phrase.*

von hier aus	from here
von jetzt an (**von nun an**)	from now on
von heute an	from today on
von Anfang an	from the beginning
von Jugend auf	from (my, his, etc.) youth (on)

D. *Study the following phrases which lack a noun object.*

auf einmal	suddenly, all at once
aufs neue	again, anew
bei weitem	by far
bis jetzt	up to now
nach vorn	forward, to the front
seit kurzem	recently, not long ago
seit wann	since when
trotz allem	in spite of everything
vor allem	above all

WRITTEN EXERCISE

1. From here one can look down into the meadow.
2. After breakfast he walked out of the inn to his car.
3. Lately he has been going to the university in the evening.
4. The family went to Munich by car yesterday.
5. The maid said they were at home after lunch.
6. In spite of the weather, he walked around the house in the rain.
7. Fortunately he stated in his letter that they were coming at six in the evening.
8. The dog ran under the tree behind the house.
9. The leaves fell from the tree beside the garden wall.
10. The student said he would walk to school with his friends.
11. The man was sitting at the table between his brothers.
12. During the day I work in the field with my uncle.
13. The teacher spoke about the countries on the map.
14. He sets the picture against the wall between the windows.
15. The boy pointed at the light over the teacher's desk.
16. Without a hat on his head, he walked through the field.
17. Two years ago he was living with my aunt without my knowing it.
18. They did it for him against my will.
19. He would come back to school for the sake of his mother if she wanted him to.
20. I am interested in the fact that you want to live in the vicinity.

LESSON 6

PERFECT TENSE FORMS

---

53) Formation

The present perfect and past perfect forms are obtained by combining the perfect participle with the present and past forms, respectively, of the required auxiliary. The perfect participle has the prefix **ge–** except with verbs of foreign origin ending in **–ieren** and with verbs having inseparable prefixes; it has the ending **–t** for weak verbs and **–en** for strong verbs.

kaufen to buy	**kauft**	**kaufte**	**hat gekauft**
schreiben to write	**schreibt**	**schrieb**	**hat geschrieben**
studieren to study	**studiert**	**studierte**	**hat studiert**
beginnen to begin	**beginnt**	**begann**	**hat begonnen**

The perfect auxiliary is either **sein** or **haben.** All transitive verbs and most intransitive verbs use **haben.** Intransitive verbs whose meaning implies change of place or condition use **sein. Sein** and **bleiben** also use **sein.**

Er ist in das Haus gelaufen.	He ran into the house.
Er hat sein Buch gelesen.	He read his book.

The auxiliary occupies the position of the finite verb as defined in the first and fourth lessons; the participle stands last in a main clause or just before the auxiliary (finite verb) in a subordinate clause.

Nachdem er sein Buch gelesen hatte, ist er in das Haus gelaufen.	After he had read his book, he ran into the house.

lesen   to read

PRESENT PERFECT

INDICATIVE	SUBJUNCTIVE (PAST I)
ich habe gelesen	ich habe gelesen
du hast gelesen	du habest gelesen
er hat gelesen	er habe gelesen
wir haben gelesen	wir haben gelesen
ihr habt gelesen	ihr habet gelesen
sie haben gelesen	sie haben gelesen

PAST PERFECT

INDICATIVE	SUBJUNCTIVE (PAST II)
ich hatte gelesen	ich hätte gelesen
du hattest gelesen	du hättest gelesen
er hatte gelesen	er hätte gelesen
wir hatten gelesen	wir hätten gelesen
ihr hattet gelesen	ihr hättet gelesen
sie hatten gelesen	sie hätten gelesen

laufen   to run, walk fast

PRESENT PERFECT

INDICATIVE	SUBJUNCTIVE (PAST I)
ich bin gelaufen	ich sei gelaufen
du bist gelaufen	du seiest gelaufen
er ist gelaufen	er sei gelaufen
wir sind gelaufen	wir seien gelaufen
ihr seid gelaufen	ihr seiet gelaufen
sie sind gelaufen	sie seien gelaufen

PAST PERFECT

INDICATIVE	SUBJUNCTIVE (PAST II)
ich war gelaufen	ich wäre gelaufen
du warst gelaufen	du wärest gelaufen
er war gelaufen	er wäre gelaufen
wir waren gelaufen	wir wären gelaufen
ihr wart gelaufen	ihr wäret gelaufen
sie waren gelaufen	sie wären gelaufen

54) The Double Infinitive

Modal auxiliaries and certain other verbs use their infinitive forms as participles when they are accompanied by complementary infinitives. These other verbs include **sehen, hören, lassen, helfen, heißen, lernen,** and **lehren.**

Wir haben nicht alles tun können.   We have not been able to do everything.

Ich habe sie oft singen hören.   I have often heard her sing.

In a subordinate clause, the double infinitive stands last with the auxiliary immediately before it.

Er sagte, daß er nicht alles habe   He said that he had not been able to
tun können.   do everything.

55) Indicative Uses

The present perfect indicative states single completed actions, whereas the simple past indicative describes progressive or repetitive actions in past time.

Wir sind in die Stadt gefahren, da   We went to town, since the sun was
die Sonne so hell schien.   shining so brightly.

The past perfect indicative describes actions in a prior past time, just as in English.

Wir waren in die Stadt gefahren,   We had gone to town before the rain
ehe der Regen begann.   began.

56) Indirect Discourse and Indirect Questions with Subjunctive Forms

In indirect discourse and indirect questions, the present perfect and past perfect subjunctive forms refer to a time prior to that referred to by the introductory verb.

Er sagte, daß er kein Geld gehabt habe.

Er sagte, daß er kein Geld gehabt hätte.
He said that he had had no money.

Er fragte, ob wir Geld gehabt hätten.
He asked whether we had had money.

Wir glaubten, daß sie schon gekommen seien.

Wir glaubten, daß sie schon gekommen wären.
We thought that they had already come.

Wir fragten, ob sie schon gekommen seien.

Wir fragten, ob sie schon gekommen wären.
We asked whether they had already come.

Subjunctive forms that sound like indicative ones are avoided in favor of unambiguous forms.

Sie sagten uns, daß sie alles getan hätten (*not* **haben**).
They told us that they had done everything.

57) Contrary-to-Fact Conditions in Past Time.*

Contrary-to-fact conditions referring to past time use past perfect subjunctive forms in both clauses.

Wenn ich das Geld gehabt hätte, wäre ich nach Europa gefahren.
If I had had the money, I would have gone to Europe.

Hätte ich das Geld gehabt, so wäre ich nach Europa gefahren.
Had I had (If I had had) the money, I would have gone to Europe.

* The **würde**-form is presented in Lesson 10.

58) Condition or Conclusion Standing Alone.*

Wenn ich nur das Geld gehabt hätte! } If I had only had the money!

Ich wäre gerne nach Europa gefahren! } I would have liked to go to Europe.

ORAL EXERCISES

A. *Conjugate in the present perfect and past perfect indicative.*

1. gehen
2. nehmen
3. finden
4. bleiben
5. antworten
6. reisen

B. *Conjugate in the present perfect and past perfect subjunctive.*

1. stehen
2. lernen
3. steigen
4. treten
5. tragen
6. reiten

C. *Translate.*

1. The milk has become warm.
2. He has gone to town.
3. If he had only been there!
4. Why had you gone?
5. I thought it had come yesterday.
6. He has heard the man sing.
7. Who had read the book?
8. He said they had caught the thief.
9. He had spoken with her.
10. Where has he been all day?

D. *Fill in the blanks with* **wann, wenn,** *or* **als. Wann** *is interrogative only;* **wenn** *equals if or when in the sense of whenever;* **als** *equals when with reference to single completed actions in past time.*

* See also section 40.

1. ____ kommt die Post?

2. ____ der Briefträger kommt, ist es elf Uhr.

3. ____ der Briefträger kam, sprach ich immer mit ihm.

4. ____ der Briefträger gestern kam, biß ihm der Hund ins Bein.

5. ____ es keine Briefträger gäbe, müßten wir die Post selbst holen.

6. Ich weiß nicht, ____ er gekommen ist.

WRITTEN EXERCISE

1. The boy cried as if the man had hit him.

2. The man said he had never seen that lady before.

3. We had discussed the matter before he had read the report.

4. If the pedestrian had not been careful, the car would have run over him.

5. They have seen your friend working in the field.

6. I would have liked to go to Germany last summer.

7. I have not yet written the sentences for this lesson.

8. He talked about his wife as if she were his worst enemy.

9. The teacher asked the student if he had understood him.

10. He would have liked the room if it had had more sunshine in the afternoon.

11. She believed that he had died last year.

12. If I had only studied diligently during the entire semester!

13. I have worked in the garden the whole day.

14. I don't remember when I have driven so far in one day.

15. The professor would have helped me yesterday anyway.

16. The man said that he had helped the lady carry her baggage.

17. I had already met my friend when I saw you yesterday.

18. The teacher asked me why I had not written the sentence on the board.

19. The woman claimed she had lost her purse in the store.

20. If only the weather had been cool!

LESSON 7

REFLEXIVE PRONOUNS

---

59) Reflexive Pronouns in English

In English, different pronouns must be used to distinguish between *he sees him* and *he sees himself* or *she likes her a lot* and *she likes herself a lot*. *He* and *him* or *she* and *her* are understood to mean different persons. The special form with the suffix *–self* represents the same person as the subject. Because it reflects back to the subject, it is called a reflexive pronoun.

60) Reflexive Pronouns in German

Because there can be no ambiguity in the first and second persons (*me* and *myself* are the same person), German uses the forms of the personal pronouns for the reflexive idea. However, in the third person and formal address a special form, **sich,** is the reflexive pronoun for all genders, for singular and plural, and for the dative and accusative cases. In formal address, **sich** is not capitalized.

The reflexive pronoun as indirect object:

Ich kaufe mir einen neuen Hut.	I am buying myself a new hat.
Du kaufst dir einen neuen Hut.	You are buying yourself a new hat.
Er kauft sich einen neuen Hut.	He is buying himself a new hat.

Sie kauft sich einen neuen Hut.	She is buying herself a new hat.
Wir kaufen uns neue Hüte.	We are buying ourselves new hats.
Ihr kauft euch neue Hüte.	You are buying yourselves new hats.
Sie kaufen sich neue Hüte.	They are buying themselves new hats.

The reflexive pronoun as direct object:

Ich sehe mich in dem Spiegel.	I see myself in the mirror.
Du siehst dich in dem Spiegel.	You see yourself in the mirror.
Er sieht sich in dem Spiegel.	He sees himself in the mirror.
Sie sieht sich in dem Spiegel.	She sees herself in the mirror.
Wir sehen uns in dem Spiegel.	We see ourselves in the mirror.
Ihr seht euch in dem Spiegel.	You see yourselves in the mirror.
Sie sehen sich in dem Spiegel.	They see themselves in the mirror.

61) Transitivity

The real problem of knowing when to use the reflexive direct object is to know whether the verb is transitive or intransitive and what kind of complements it takes. A transitive verb is defined as one that requires a direct object.

Many English verbs are used both ways:

Papers burn (*intransitive*).	A person burns his papers (*transitive*).
An idea develops (*intransitive*).	A photographer develops a film (*transitive*).

Fewer German verbs vary between transitive and intransitive meaning. This fact causes the reflexive object to appear more often in German than in English. **Ich wasche mich.** *I am washing.* The German **waschen** is transitive, and therefore incomplete without a direct object. The English *wash* is intransitive in the meaning intended here. But in both languages, this verb can take a wide range of objects having nothing to do with reflexive meaning.

Ich wasche das Auto (den Boden, das Geschirr).	I am washing the car (the floor, the dishes).

Many transitive verbs, like **waschen,** take either reflexive or other objects:

Ich amüsierte mich.	I had a good time.
Ich amüsierte meine Freunde.	I entertained (amused) my friends.
Du ärgertest dich.	You got angry.

Du ärgertest den Lehrer.	You made the teacher angry.
Die Erde dreht sich um ihre Achse.	The earth revolves on its axis.
Ich kann den Türgriff nicht drehen.	I can't turn the doorknob.

62) Some transitive verbs are purely reflexive; that is, their meaning would hardly permit any object other than a reflexive one.

Ich habe mich ausgeruht.	I have had a good rest.
Er beeilt sich.	He is hurrying.

63) A few transitive verbs are normally accompanied by a reflexive indirect object.

Willst du dir das Zimmer ansehen?	Do you want to see the room (take a look at the room for yourself)?
Ich kann mir den großen Schaden nicht vorstellen.	I can't imagine (picture to myself) the tremendous destruction (damage).

64) Reciprocal Meaning of the Reflexive Pronoun

In the plural, the reflexive pronoun also has a reciprocal meaning equal to **einander** *each other.*

Wir sehen uns (einander) bald wieder.	We will soon meet (see each other, one another) again.
Sie geben sich (einander) die Hände.	They shake hands.

ORAL EXERCISES

A. *Study the following verbs, which always have, for the meanings indicated, a reflexive direct object.*

sich anziehen (ausziehen) draw pull

Die Kinder ziehen sich nicht schnell an (aus).

Children do not dress (undress) quickly.

sich ausruhen	**Haben Sie sich ausgeruht?**
	Have you had a good rest?
sich bedanken	**Ich habe mich bei ihm für seine Hilfe bedankt.**
	I have expressed my thanks to him for his assistance.
sich beeilen	**Beeile dich!**
	Hurry up!
sich befinden	**Ich befand mich mitten auf der Straße.**
	I was (found myself) in the middle of the street.
sich benehmen (betragen)	**Das Kind benimmt (beträgt) sich sehr fein.**
	The child behaves very well.
sich bewerben	**Du solltest dich um eine neue Stellung bewerben.**
	You should apply for a new job.
sich bücken	**Wir bückten uns und sammelten die Papiere.**
	We bent down (stooped) and gathered the papers.
sich entscheiden	**Das Gericht hat sich für Sie entschieden.**
	The court has decided in your favor.
sich erholen (von)	**Von den Masern erholt man sich schnell.**
	People recover quickly from measles.
sich erkälten	**Hast du dich erkältet?**
	Did you catch a cold?

sich erkundigen	**Habt ihr euch nach dem Kranken erkundigt?**
inquire	Did you inquire about the sick man?
sich fühlen	**Ich fühle mich heute besser als gestern.**
feel (happy etc)	I feel better today than yesterday.
sich gewöhnen	**Die Menschen gewöhnen sich an alles.**
accustom	People become accustomed to anything.
sich kümmern (um)	**Kümmern Sie sich nicht zuviel darum!**
worry	Don't worry too much about it.
sich nähern (+ *indirect object*)	**Die Katze näherte sich dem Vogel.**
approach	The cat approached the bird.
sich räuspern	**Der Sänger mußte sich räuspern.**
clear one's throat	The singer had to clear his throat.
sich schämen (+ *genitive or* **wegen** + *genitive*)	**Der Junge schämte sich (wegen) seiner alten Schuhe vor seinen Freunden.**
be ashamed	The boy was ashamed of his old shoes in the presence of his friends.
sich sehnen (nach)	**Sehnst du dich nach deiner alten Heimat?**
long for	Are you longing for your former home?
sich tasten	**Weil es keinen Strom gab, mußten wir uns durch das Haus tasten.**
feel	Because there was no electricity, we had to feel our way through the house.

sich üben (in + *dative*) *[excercise practice]*	**Du solltest dich im Klavierspielen üben.**
	You should practice playing the piano.
sich verbeugen *[bow]*	**Verbeugt man sich immer vor der Königin?**
	Do you always bow to the Queen?
sich verirren *[lose one's way]*	**Die Kinder könnten sich im Wald verirren.**
	The children could lose their way (get lost) in the woods.
sich verlassen (auf + *accusative*) *[rely on - depend]*	**Auf wen kannst du dich verlassen?**
	On whom can you depend?
sich wundern (über + *accusative*) *[surprised wonder]*	**Wir wundern uns über den Preis des Wagens.**
	We are surprised at the price of the car.

B. *Study the following transitive verbs, which require a reflexive indirect object for the meanings indicated.*

sich ansehen *[look at regard]*	**Ich möchte mir dieses Bild ansehen.**
	I would like to look at this picture.
sich leisten *[afford do, perform]*	**Ich kann mir kein neues Auto leisten.**
	I can't afford a new car.
sich vorstellen *[imagine]*	**Stellen Sie sich** (*dative*) **die Landschaft vor!**
	Imagine (picture) the landscape.

C. The following verbs can take a variety of objects other than reflexive pronouns. *Form short statements with* (1) *a reflexive object and* (2) *an object other than reflexive.*

Example: **ankleiden**   to dress.

> **Ich kleide mich an.**   I dress (myself).
>
> **Die Mutter kleidet das**   The mother dresses the baby.
> **Kind an.**

1. **amüsieren** amuse, entertain; *refl.* have a good time
2. **ärgern** (**über** + *acc.*) annoy, irritate; *refl.* be annoyed (at)
3. **bewegen** move (*change of location, not change of residence*)
4. **(um)drehen** turn (around); *refl.* revolve
5. **entwickeln** develop
6. **erinnern** (**an** + *acc.*) remind (of); *refl.* remember
7. **freuen** please; *refl.* be pleased, be glad
   sich freuen auf + *acc.* look forward to
   sich freuen über + *acc.* rejoice at, be pleased with
8. **fürchten** fear; *refl.* (+ **vor** + *dat.*) be afraid (of)
9. **interessieren** interest; *refl.* (+ **für**) be (become) interested (in)
10. **setzen** place, set; *refl.* sit down
11. **verändern** change
12. **vorstellen** (+ *ind. and dir. objects*) introduce
13. **waschen** wash
14. **wenden** turn

D. *Conjugate in the present, simple past, perfect, and past perfect tenses.*

1. Ich kaufe mir heute nichts.
2. Ich verlasse mich auf meinen Freund.
3. Ich freue mich auf die Ferien.

WRITTEN EXERCISE

1. I saw you in the picture. Do you see yourself in it?
2. If we hurry, we can apply for a job today.
3. What would you do if you lost your way in a strange city?
4. Grandfather does not feel well today; he has caught a cold.
5. When the ship approaches the harbor, the travelers are always surprised at the tall buildings.
6. Have you introduced yourself to your new neighbor?
7. Do all the planets revolve on (around) their axes?
8. My younger brother has become interested in astronomy.
9. If the child were afraid of the dog, he would scream.
10. When you become accustomed to the reflexive pronoun, you are no longer annoyed at it.
11. Look at this old car; you don't have to bend down to climb into it.
12. I will remind her of the words once more, and then she should remember them.
13. Everybody had a good time at our party.
14. Languages change constantly, but we have not changed our orthography for a long time.
15. As we were inquiring about our former teacher, he approached us.
16. I can well imagine that you are looking forward to your trip.
17. Men do not bow any more; they shake hands.
18. Have you decided to take a trip next year?
19. The policeman turned around and inquired about the driver of the car.
20. If you leaned out the window, you could see the brook on the left.

LESSON 8

VERB PREFIXES

---

65) Prefixes in English

In English the difference in meaning is apparent between *set up* and *upset,* *run over* and *overrun, look over* and *overlook.* The first of each pair is a combination of a verb with a modifier; the second is a combination of a verb with a prefix that always remains attached. The former combination retains the basic meaning of the verb, but the latter often produces a different, perhaps unexpected, meaning. Also the stress pattern is consistent: the modifier receives greater stress than the verb, but the verb stem is stressed in the inseparable combinations.

√ 66) Inseparable Prefixes

Learn These

Inseparable prefixes function in German in the same manner as in English. The verb stem is always stressed, and the participle does not add a **ge-** prefix.

Seven prefixes are always inseparable.

be-	**bestellen** to order	**bestellt**	**bestellte**	**hat bestellt**
emp-	**empfehlen** to recommend	**empfiehlt**	**empfahl**	**hat empfohlen**
ent-	**entlaufen** to escape	**entläuft**	**entlief**	**ist entlaufen**
er-	**erfahren** to experience	**erfährt**	**erfuhr**	**hat erfahren**
ge-	**geschehen** to happen	**geschieht**	**geschah**	**ist geschehen**
ver-	**versprechen** to promise	**verspricht**	**versprach**	**hat versprochen**
zer-	**zerreißen** to tear to bits	**zerreißt**	**zerriß**	**hat zerrissen**

√64

67) Separable Prefixes

The separable prefixes may be understood as adverbs which are always placed at the end of a main clause or attached to infinitives and participles. They are not separated from the simple tense forms in subordinate clauses. Separable prefixes are always stressed.

aufstehen to get up **steht ... auf**	**stand ... auf ist aufgestanden**
Er steht immer früh auf.	He always gets up early.
Er muß immer früh aufstehen.	He always has to get up early.
Er sagte, daß er immer früh aufstehe.	He said that he always got up (gets up) early.

68) Variable Prefixes

The prefixes **durch, hinter, über, um, unter, voll, wider,** and **wieder** occur in both patterns. With **durch, voll,** and **wider,** a variation in meaning cannot easily be discerned.

Setzen Sie mich über den Fluß hinüber!	Take me across the river.
Übersetzen Sie Ihre Aufgabe!	Translate your assignment.
Die Töne widerhallen. ⎫ **Die Töne hallen wider.** ⎭	The sounds (tones) echo.

69) hin and her

Hin and **her** indicate respectively direction away from and toward the speaker or point of reference. They are often attached to other prefixes.

Kommen Sie her!	Come (over) here.
Kommen Sie herein!	Come in (here).
Der Hund will hinaus.	The dog wants (to go) out.

70) wo, woher, wohin

The interrogative adverbs **wo, woher,** and **wohin** have different meanings.

Wo hält der Autobus?	Where (at what place) does the bus stop?

Woher kommt dieser Autobus? ⎫	
Wo kommt dieser Autobus her? ⎭	Where does this bus come from?
Wohin fährt dieser Autobus? ⎫	Where (to what place) does this bus
Wo fährt dieser Autobus hin? ⎭	go?

71) Combinations of Prepositions and Prefixes

The functional distinction between prepositions and prefixes frequently demands the use of both to satisfy syntactical requirements.

Die Kinder laufen um den Baum herum.	The children are running around the tree.
Jetzt laufen sie in das Haus hinein.	Now they are running into the house.

ORAL EXERCISES

A. *Conjugate the following verbs in the present, past, present perfect, and past perfect indicative tenses.*

1. beginnen
2. ankommen
3. verstehen
4. eintreten
5. zerbrechen
6. mitbringen

B. *Translate.*

1. The train leaves at six.
2. Who discovered America?
3. I have explained it.
4. What had happened?
5. She went and got it again.
6. I have described her.
7. When had the class started?
8. Who invited them?
9. He has just translated the word.
10. He brought the book along.

WRITTEN EXERCISE

Do these

1. The man paid the check when he was leaving the restaurant.

2. The teacher reminded me of my homework and then disappeared from the classroom.

3. The servant would not have opened the windows if the wind had started to blow.

4. I have learned (found out) that her friend returned from a trip last week.

5. The sun was just rising when we reached the top of the mountain.

6. He had expected a letter yesterday and could not understand why he did not receive one.

7. The dog had torn the cloth to pieces before the woman could take it away.

8. The children had forgotten that they had told the same story last week.

9. The lady disappeared in the crowd just as I recognized her.

10. I do not remember on which page we stopped yesterday.

11. Although most people got up and left, he continued with his speech.

12. My brother ran away when I came out of the house.

13. We got up rather early this morning in order to arrive at our destination before noon.

14. He had decided to go home, since he had caught a cold.

15. They have recommended this car because it has received the first prize.

16. The car was surrounded by beautiful ladies before the driver was able to get out.

17. The sun set behind the mountains after the boys had conversed about half an hour.

18. We were enjoying the beautiful scenery when the accident happened.

19. His wife went into the kitchen and put the plates down on the table.

20. They told us that they had spent their vacation at the lake and had arrived home late in the afternoon.

LESSON 9

---

72) The **der-**words and the **ein-**words have the endings **–e,** **–er, –en, –e** for all genders in the plural.

73) **der-**words, **ein-**words and Noun Declension in the Plural

The nominative plural of every German noun must be learned individually. From it, the rest of the plural declension can be produced. All nouns have an **–n** in the dative plural except those with **–s** plurals.

N. **die Freunde**	**solche Wagen**	**keine Bücher**	**uns(e)re Autos**
G. **der Freunde**	**solcher Wagen**	**keiner Bücher**	**uns(e)rer Autos**
D. **den Freunden**	**solchen Wagen**	**keinen Büchern**	**uns(e)ren Autos**
A. **die Freunde**	**solche Wagen**	**keine Bücher**	**uns(e)re Autos**

74) -en Plurals

A. All feminine polysyllables, except **die Mutter** and **die Tochter,** and all feminine monosyllables except about forty form their plurals with **–n** or **–en.**

die Blume	flower	**die Blumen**
die Feder	pen, feather	**die Federn**
die Frau	woman, wife	**die Frauen**
die Freundin	friend	**die Freundinnen**

68

B. Masculine nouns with a genitive singular in **–en** form their plurals with **–en**. Those of recent foreign origin are recognized by a stress on the final syllable of the nominative singular.

der **Junge** boy	des **Jungen**	die **Jungen**
der **Student** student	des **Studenten**	die **Studenten**
der **Preuße** Prussian	des **Preußen**	die **Preußen**
der **Neffe** nephew	des **Neffen**	die **Neffen**
der **Löwe** lion	des **Löwen**	die **Löwen**

C. Foreign masculine nouns with a change of stress between singular and plural have **–s** in the genitive singular and **–en** in the plural. A few native masculine and neuter nouns are declined similarly.

der **Dóktor** doctor, Ph.D.	des **Dóktors**	die **Doktóren**
der **Proféssor** professor	des **Proféssors**	die **Professóren**
der **Staat** state, country	des **Staates**	die **Staaten**
der **Bauer** farmer	des **Bauers** *or* **Bauern**	die **Bauern**
der **Vetter** cousin	des **Vetters**	die **Vettern**
das **Auge** eye	des **Auges**	die **Augen**
das **Ohr** ear	des **Ohres**	die **Ohren**
das **Ende** end	des **Endes**	die **Enden**
das **Bett** bed	des **Bettes**	die **Betten**

75) Plural Forms without Endings

A. Most masculine and neuter polysyllables ending in **–el, –en,** or **–er** have the same form in the nominative plural as in the singular except that some of these umlaut the stem vowel. Collectives with the prefix **Ge–** and the suffix **–e** always have the same vowel in singular and plural.

der **Wagen** car, coach, wagon	die **Wagen**
der **Vater** father	die **Väter**
das **Fenster** window	die **Fenster**
das **Gebäude** building	die **Gebäude**

B. All diminutives have the same form in singular and plural.

das **Fräulein** young woman	die **Fräulein**
das **Mädchen** girl	die **Mädchen**
das **Büchlein** little book	die **Büchlein**

C. Three feminine nouns do not add endings.

die **Mutter** mother	die **Mütter**
die **Tochter** daughter	die **Töchter**
die **Mark** mark (*unit of currency*)	die **Mark**

76) -e Plurals

A. Most masculine monosyllables and a few neuter monosyllables add **–e** in the plural. Most of the masculine ones umlaut; the neuter ones do not umlaut.

der **Stuhl** chair	die **Stühle**
der **Freund** friend	die **Freunde**
der **Kopf** head	die **Köpfe**
das **Brot** (loaf of) bread	die **Brote**
der **Hut** hat	die **Hüte**

B. The feminine monosyllables that do not have **–en** plurals add **–e** and always umlaut their stem vowels. There are only about forty of these.

die **Hand** hand	die **Hände**
die **Kuh** cow	die **Kühe**
die **Braut** fiancée	die **Bräute**
die **Nacht** night	die **Nächte**

C. Masculine and neuter polysyllables not described under 74 belong to the **e**-plural category.

der **König** king	die **Könige**
der **Sperling** sparrow	die **Sperlinge**
das **Gesetz** law	die **Gesetze**
der **Monat** month	die **Monate**
das **Schicksal** destiny	die **Schicksale**
das **Gefängnis** prison	die **Gefängnisse**

77) -er Plurals

A. Most neuter monosyllables and a few masculine monosyllables belong to the **–er**-plural category. They umlaut their stem vowels if possible.

das **Buch** book	die **Bücher**
das **Bild** picture	die **Bilder**
der **Gott** God, god	die **Götter**
der **Mann** man	die **Männer**
der **Wald** forest	die **Wälder**

B. Masculine and neuter nouns with the suffix **–tum** umlaut the suffix and add **–er.**

das **Herzogtum** duchy	die **Herzogtümer**
der **Irrtum** error	die **Irrtümer**

C. A few neuter nouns with the prefix **Ge–** belong to the **–er** category.

das **Gehalt** salary	die **Gehälter**
das **Gemach** room	die **Gemächer**

78) Variable Plurals

Some nouns have variable plurals, which may reflect variations of meaning.

der **Band** volume, book	die **Bände**
das **Band** tie, bond	die **Bande**
das **Band** ribbon	die **Bänder**
das **Gesicht** vision	die **Gesichte**
das **Gesicht** face	die **Gesichter**
das **Wort** word	die **Worte** words (*in context*)
das **Wort** word	die **Wörter** (*separate*) words; cf. **Wörterbuch**

79) Nouns of Measure

Masculine and neuter nouns of measure use the singular form as a plural when they are preceded by a number; feminine nouns of measure ending in **–e** use their plural forms.

drei **Glas Bier**	three glasses of beer
zwei **Pfund Käse**	two pounds of cheese
zwei **Paar Schuhe**	two pairs of shoes
vier **Tassen Kaffee**	four cups of coffee

80) Compound Nouns

In compound nouns, the last element determines the gender and declensional pattern.

die Kirche church + **das Fenster** window = **das Kirchenfenster** church window

der Flug flight + **das Zeug** tool = **das Flugzeug** airplane

ORAL EXERCISE

Decline in singular and plural.

1. der Affe	11. das Kätzchen
2. mein Arm	12. dieses Kino
3. jedes Blatt	13. unser Klassenzimmer
4. der Direktor	14. welcher Mann
5. ein Franzose	15. seine Schwester
6. die Französin	16. jener Stuhl
7. der Gedanke	17. diese Stunde
8. mancher Geist	18. welches Tischbein
9. ihr Gemälde	19. euer Großvater
10. deine Hand	20. unsere Wandtafel

WRITTEN EXERCISE

1. One must learn the plural forms of nouns individually.
2. American students sometimes do not understand that cinemas and theaters are different things.
3. What wild animals do you find in the United States?
4. There are bears, rabbits, wolves, and beavers here.
5. In Africa you could see lions, monkeys, elephants, and giraffes.

6. My brother's sons and daughters are the cousins (*m.* + *f.*) of my children.

7. The answers to some questions cannot be found in these books.

8. We look up the explanations of words in dictionaries.

9. Are the words *To be or not to be* familiar to you?

10. The two little boys clenched their fists and hit each other before their mothers could seize them.

11. How many newspapers and magazines does our library receive?

12. The days of the week and the months of the year have masculine names in German.

13. Place your papers and pencils on your desks when you leave the room.

14. If the earth had nine moons, the nights would never be dark.

15. Do you learn more through your eyes or through your ears?

16. In the next few days, our class will visit the museum to see paintings from past centuries.

17. Do trains stop only in the big cities or in the small towns too?

18. The girls are placing glasses and cups on the tables.

19. All students must pronounce the new sounds of foreign languages again and again.

20. The student said he had decided to write these sentences carefully.

LESSON 10

FUTURE TENSE FORMS

81) Formation

The future and future perfect forms are obtained by combining the auxiliary **werden** with the present and perfect infinitives, respectively. Where the indicative has two future tenses using the present forms of **werden,** the subjunctive has four forms, because two extra ones are built with the past forms of the auxiliary.

FUTURE INDICATIVE	FUTURE SUBJUNCTIVE (FUTURE I)	PRESENT CONDITIONAL (FUTURE II)
ich werde machen	ich werde machen	ich würde machen
du wirst machen	du werdest machen	du würdest machen
er wird machen	er werde machen	er würde machen
wir werden machen	wir werden machen	wir würden machen
ihr werdet machen	ihr werdet machen	ihr würdet machen
sie werden machen	sie werden machen	sie würden machen

FUTURE PERFECT INDIC.	FUTURE PERFECT SUBJUNC. (FUTURE PERFECT I)
ich werde gemacht haben	ich werde gemacht haben
du wirst gemacht haben	du werdest gemacht haben
er wird gemacht haben	er werde gemacht haben
wir werden gemacht haben	wir werden gemacht haben
ihr werdet gemacht haben	ihr werdet gemacht haben
sie werden gemacht haben	sie werden gemacht haben

PAST CONDITIONAL
(FUTURE PERFECT II)

ich würde gemacht haben
du würdest gemacht haben
er würde gemacht haben
wir würden gemacht haben
ihr würdet gemacht haben
sie würden gemacht haben

Present [handwritten] Ich schreibe einen Brief
Passive voice [handwritten] Der Brief wird von mir geschrieben

82) Indicative Uses

The future and future perfect tenses may have the same meaning as the corresponding English forms.

Er wird nächste Woche hier sein.	He will be here next week.
Man wird das neue Gebäude schon gebaut haben, ehe wir wieder zur Universität zurückkehren.	The new building will have been built before we return to the university.

The future tense also indicates probability or an assumption referring to present time, and the future perfect indicates probability or an assumption referring to past time. Frequently the modifier **wohl** emphasizes this interpretation.

Unsere Freunde werden wohl zu Hause sein.	Our friends are probably at home. (*That is, we will probably find out, if we inquire, that they are at home.*)
Sie werden den Film wohl gesehen haben.	They have probably seen the film. (*That is, we will probably discover that they have already seen the film.*)

83) würde-forms in Contrary-to-Fact Conditions

In the conclusion (main clause) of a condition contrary-to-fact in present time, the form **würde fahren,** which is called the present conditional, is an alternate form for the past subjunctive **führe.** Likewise the past conditional, **würde gefahren sein,** is an alternate for the past perfect subjunctive **wäre gefahren** in the conclusion of a past condition contrary-to-fact.

**Wenn ich das Geld hätte, dann
    führe ich nach Europa.**
**Wenn ich das Geld hätte, dann
    würde ich nach Europa fahren.**

If I had the money, I would go to Europe.

**Wenn ich das Geld gehabt hätte,
    so wäre ich nach Europa gefahren.**
**Wenn ich das Geld gehabt hätte,
    so würde ich nach Europa gefahren sein.**

If I had had the money, I would have gone to Europe.

84) Indirect Discourse

The future subjunctive and present conditional forms indicate a temporal relationship subsequent to the time of the introductory verb.

Er sagte, daß er kein Geld haben werde.
Er sagte, daß er kein Geld haben würde.
Er sagte, er werde (würde) kein Geld haben.

He said that he would have no money.

The future perfect subjunctive and past conditional forms rarely occur in indirect discourse.

Er sagte, daß er kein Geld gehabt haben werde.
Er sagte, daß er kein Geld gehabt haben würde.
Er sagte, er werde (würde) kein Geld gehabt haben.

He said that he would have had no money.

ORAL EXERCISES

A. *Conjugate in the future and future perfect indicative.*

1. gehen
2. annehmen
3. finden
4. bleiben
5. beantworten
6. reisen

B. *Conjugate in the future subjunctive (future I), present conditional (future II), future perfect subjunctive (future perfect I), and past conditional (future perfect II).*

1. entstehen
2. lernen
3. steigen
4. eintreten
5. tragen
6. reiten

C. A synopsis is the set of verb forms for one person in each of the tenses. In the indicative synopsis there are six forms and in the subjunctive synopsis eight forms.

1. *Give a synopsis in the third person singular, indicative mood, active voice, of each verb in Exercise A.*
2. *Give a synopsis in the third person singular, subjunctive mood, active voice, of each verb in Exercise B.*

D. *Translate.*

1. Where will you be tomorrow?
2. The students will write their lessons.
3. He will have gone home before evening.
4. She wrote that she would come tomorrow.
5. Our friends would have had a good time at the party.
6. They have probably gone to the movie.
7. I will have finished my homework in an hour.
8. He would have done it if he had had the time.
9. The lady said she would be here on time.
10. The teachers are probably sleeping too late.

WRITTEN EXERCISE

1. We will have spent all our money by tomorrow if we are not a bit more thrifty.
2. He has probably gone home, since he suddenly got sick after dinner.
3. The newspaper reported that a famous poet will arrive by train tomorrow.
4. If she could have read the German book, she would have done it long ago.
5. He will go home next week and report about these conditions.
6. The thief would be asked again and again whether he had said he didn't know where the money was hidden.
7. The teacher said that every person would buy the books of the famous poet who had just died.
8. If he had more patience, his work would be more successful.
9. The mother would have read more fairy tales to the children if they had listened attentively.
10. The merchant considered how he could sell his merchandise best.
11. I asked the farmer if he had offered the stranger a glass of water.
12. Had the students been more attentive, they would not have made so many mistakes.
13. In July, the weather will probably be hot and get hotter every day.
14. He has probably studied German more diligently than anyone else in the class.
15. I would not have worried about my friends if they had not arrived late.
16. When I meet them next week, they will already have spent two weeks of their vacation.
17. The mother wrote the teacher that she should excuse her son because he had been sick.
18. Many mothers will write the previous sentence as an excuse for their children during the coming months.
19. Next month we will buy mother a dress as a present for her birthday.
20. He would come back to our city if he were promised a better position.

LESSON 11

ADJECTIVE ENDINGS

85) Adjective Declension after **der**-words (Weak Declension)

The **der**-words, having the most nearly perfect set of endings, take the full responsibility of indicating gender, number, and case; hence, any **ein**-word or attributive adjective following a **der**-word uses a simplified set of endings consisting of **–e** in five forms and of **–en** in all others.

M.	F.	N.
N. der braune Tisch	diese kleine Tasche	das schöne Mädchen
G. des braunen Tisches	dieser kleinen Tasche	des schönen Mädchens
D. dem braunen Tisch(e)	dieser kleinen Tasche	dem schönen Mädchen
A. den braunen Tisch	diese kleine Tasche	das schöne Mädchen

PL.

N. die braunen Tische	diese kleinen Taschen	die schönen Mädchen
G. der braunen Tische	dieser kleinen Taschen	der schönen Mädchen
D. den braunen Tischen	diesen kleinen Taschen	den schönen Mädchen
A. die braunen Tische	diese kleinen Taschen	die schönen Mädchen

Adjectives following **alle** and **beide** have the same endings as adjectives following **der**-words.

PL.

N. alle braunen Tische
G. aller braunen Tische
D. allen braunen Tischen
A. alle braunen Tische

Derjenige, diejenige, dasjenige (*that, that one*) and **derselbe, dieselbe, dasselbe** (*the same*) are written as one word, although both parts are declined.

	N.	PL.
N.	dasselbe Buch	dieselben Bücher
G.	desselben Buches	derselben Bücher
D.	demselben Buch(e)	denselben Büchern
A.	dasselbe Buch	dieselben Bücher

86) Adjective Declension after **ein**-words (Mixed Declension)

Ein-words vary from **der**-words in that they lack endings in the masculine nominative singular and the neuter nominative and accusative singular. Therefore the attributive adjective following an **ein**-word must supply the distinctive endings in these cases.

M.	F.	N.
N. kein brauner Tisch	meine leere Tasche	unser offenes Fenster
G. keines braunen Tisches	meiner leeren Tasche	uns(e)res offenen Fensters
D. keinem braunen Tisch(e)	meiner leeren Tasche	uns(e)rem offenen Fenster
A. keinen braunen Tisch	meine leere Tasche	unser offenes Fenster

PL.

N. keine braunen Tische	meine leeren Taschen	uns(e)re offenen Fenster
G. keiner braunen Tische	meiner leeren Taschen	uns(e)rer offenen Fenster
D. keinen braunen Tischen	meinen leeren Taschen	uns(e)ren offenen Fenstern
A. keine braunen Tische	meine leeren Taschen	uns(e)re offenen Fenster

87) Adjective Declension Not Preceded by **der-** or **ein-**words (Strong Declension)

In the absence of a **der-** or **ein-**word, the attributive adjective must take full responsibility for identifying gender, number, and case except in the masculine and neuter genitive singular, where the **–s** of the noun identifies the case.

	M.	F.	N.
N.	roter Wein	heiße Suppe	grünes Glas
G.	roten Weines	heißer Suppe	grünen Glases
D.	rotem Wein(e)	heißer Suppe	grünem Glas(e)
A.	roten Wein	heiße Suppe	grünes Glas

PL.

N.	rote Weine	heiße Suppen	grüne Gläser
G.	roter Weine	heißer Suppen	grüner Gläser
D.	roten Weinen	heißen Suppen	grünen Gläsern
A.	rote Weine	heiße Suppen	grüne Gläser

88) Adjectives as Nouns

When an adjective serves as a noun, the adjective has a capital letter and a declensional ending.

der Alte	the old man	**das Schöne**	the beautiful
die Alte	the old woman	**das Gute**	the good
der Reiche	the rich man	**etwas Gutes**	something good
ein Reicher	a rich man	**alles Gute**	everything good
die Meinigen	my own (people, family)		

89) Attributive adjectives in a series have the same endings and are separated by commas.

ein großes, weißes Haus   a big white house

90) Demonstrative forms denoting possession and referring to previously mentioned nouns exist in the forms **meiner, der meine,** and **der meinige.**

Wessen Bleistift ist das?	Whose pencil is that?
Das ist meiner.	
Das ist der meine.	It is mine.
Das ist der meinige.	

91) When a **der**-word and an **ein**-word modify the same noun, the second in order is treated as a descriptive adjective.

N.	**ein jeder Mann** each man	**der eine Mann** the one man	
G.	**eines jeden Mannes**	**des einen Mannes**	
D.	**einem jeden Mann(e)**	**dem einen Mann(e)**	
A.	**einen jeden Mann**	**den einen Mann**	

92) Adjectives ending in **–el** drop the **e** when endings are added. Adjectives in **–en** and **–er** normally retain the **e**.

eine dunkle Nacht	a dark night
die innere Stimme	the inner voice
ein goldener Ring	a gold ring

93) Undeclined Modifiers

Noun modifiers that do not take endings include the cardinal numerals (except **ein**), the indeclinable forms **mehr** (*more*), **etwas** (*some*), **genug** (*enough*), **ein paar** (*a few*), **rosa** (*rose*), **lila** (*lilac, violet*), and modifiers with the suffix **–lei: allerlei** (*all kinds of*), **vielerlei** (*many kinds of*), etc. **Viel** (*much*) and **wenig** (*little, a little*) commonly lack endings before singular nouns.

Ich habe nur ein paar Autos auf der Straße gesehen.	I saw only a few cars on the street.
Die Kinder stellen vielerlei (mancherlei) Fragen.	Children ask many kinds of questions.
Das macht uns viel Mühe.	That causes us a lot of trouble.
Exception: **Vielen Dank!**	Many thanks (thanks very much).

94) Descriptive adjectives have a special pattern after the following modifiers denoting indefinite quantities: **andere** (*other, different*), **einige** (*some*), **etliche** (*some*), **manche** (*some*), **mehrere** (*several*), **viele** (*many*), and **wenige** (*few*).

N.	**einige gute Menschen**
G.	**einiger guten Menschen**
D.	**einigen guten Menschen**
A.	**einige gute Menschen**

95) Attributive adjectives formed from names of cities by adding the suffix **–er** are indeclinable.

Das ist eine Berliner Zeitung.	That is a Berlin newspaper.
Die Reklamen einer Berliner Zeitung sind höchst interessant.	The advertisements of (in) a Berlin newspaper are most interesting.
In einer Berliner Zeitung gibt es vieles über die Politik.	In a Berlin paper there is a lot about politics.

96) **Hoch** loses its **ch**-sound before endings.

die hohen Bäume   the tall trees

97) Predicate adjectives do not take endings.

Jene Bäume sind alt.   Those trees are old.

ORAL EXERCISES

A. *Decline in the singular and plural in German.*

1. fresh egg
2. our new car
3. that old book

4. white wine
5. which big map
6. no diligent student

B. *Translate.*

1. young people
2. a crooked leg
3. of those green vegetables
4. in her tight shoes
5. of the proud father
6. with all our friends
7. for your little brother
8. in no way
9. of a big dog
10. on the same slow train
11. with strong hands
12. through the tall windows
13. of fresh cold water
14. tall handsome prince
15. into a nice warm room
16. of white snow
17. out of a tall green tree
18. the fresh black bread
19. with a long sharp knife
20. because of an agreeable smile

WRITTEN EXERCISE

1. A bright moon was shining on that beautiful evening when we became acquainted with each other.

2. We lived on an old narrow street with many old, tall, beautiful buildings.

3. This handsome prince has said all kinds of nice things about the cheerful young lady.

4. The farmer said that he had heard nothing good about that strange person.

5. The noble knight, who was a very good and brave man, was always ready to help the poor and the weak.

6. If the same student had had enough time last year, he would have read several good books about German literature.

7. Although a few yellow leaves were hanging on the trees, deep snow lay everywhere on the ground.

8. The men all had black beards and smoked long pipes.

9. Pretty shrubs and tall trees stood on both sides of the garden.

10. Last night we slept outside in the fresh air.

11. That rich traveler has bought all kinds of beautiful pictures by great painters.
12. Lovers of German music can be found everywhere.
13. The stern teacher told the angry parents that their children had forgotten several important things.
14. Our rich uncle built himself a new house in the vicinity of a small lake.
15. The old Viennese customs are described sufficiently in this well-written book.
16. They had caught the wounded animal in the big field behind the white house.
17. The father gave his watch to the one son and his ring to the other.
18. Whose old car is standing under our big tree? It is his.
19. Yesterday I went for a short walk in our beautiful park with my two friends.
20. We have to learn the irregular forms of the strong verbs and the nouns with the definite article.

LESSON 12

SPECIAL USES OF CASES

98) The Dative Idea

Many uses of the dative case trouble the English-speaking person because the effect of the dative form is for him a new concept. The occurrences depending on prepositions and those identifiable as indirect objects are easily described. However, many other occurrences of dative forms must be described from some other viewpoint.

We can say that a dative form in context always establishes a reference to some other word, which may be a verb, noun, adjective, or adverb. The question of what a dative form relates to or refers to can bring out the meaning of the context.

Ich folge dem Mann = Ich folge, wohin der Mann geht.   I follow the man = I follow wherever the man goes.

Folgen is intransitive like **gehen.** The dative form shows that the action is performed with some relation to **dem Mann.**

99) Intransitive Verbs with Dative Forms as Sole Complements

A large number of intransitive verbs take a complement in the dative case.

Drohen Sie mir nicht!   Don't threaten me.
Das Kind ähnelt der Mutter.   The child resembles his (her) mother.

Der Knecht dient seinem Herrn treu.	The servant serves his master faithfully.
Ich helfe Ihnen, wenn Sie wollen.	I'll help you, if you want (me to).
Ich bin meinem Nachbar(n) auf der Straße begegnet.	I met my neighbor on the street.
Es fehlt mir an Geld. (Mir fehlt Geld.)	I lack money.
Du hast mir sehr gefehlt.	I have missed you very much. (You have been absent from me.)

The following common verbs take a dative complement.

ähneln	resemble	**gelingen**	succeed, be successful (for)
begegnen	meet, encounter		
beiwohnen	attend, be present at	**genügen**	suffice, be sufficient
danken	thank		
dienen	serve	**gleichen**	(be) equal (to), resemble
drohen	threaten		
einfallen	occur (to one's mind)	**gratulieren (zu)**	congratulate (on)
entfliehen	flee, escape (from)	**helfen**	help
entgehen	escape (from)	**nützen**	be useful (to)
entkommen	escape (from)	**passen**	(be) fit, suit
entsprechen	correspond (to)	**schaden**	harm
fehlen	be lacking	**schmecken**	taste, taste good (to)
folgen	follow, obey		
gefallen	please, be pleasing (to)	**schmeicheln**	flatter
		trauen	trust
gehorchen	obey	**widersprechen**	contradict
gehören	belong to		

100) antworten and glauben

The dative complements of **antworten** and **glauben** are really indirect objects, since these verbs can also have direct objects.

Was hat er dir geantwortet?	What did he answer you?
Er hat mir kein Wort geantwortet.	He didn't answer me a word.
Ich glaube dir alles = Ich glaube alles, was du sagst.	I believe everything you say.
Ich glaube ihm nichts.	I don't believe anything he says.

101) Dative Relationships to Nouns

Dative forms associated with nouns may identify the possessor of the thing or the person concerned with or affected by the thing.

Das schien mir ein Rätsel.	That seemed puzzling (a puzzle) to me.
Dies ist den Studenten ein neuer Gedanke.	This is a new idea to the students.
Er wäscht sich die Hände.	He is washing his hands.
Das war ihnen eine Freude.	That was a joy to them.
Man sieht es dir an den Augen an.	I (we) can see it in your eyes (tell by looking at your eyes).
Er ist uns in den Weg getreten.	He stepped into our path (way).

102) Adjectives with Dative Complements

Frequently the dative form is clearly understandable as dependent upon an adjective. Less often it is dependent upon an adverb.

Das Kleid ist ihr zu lang.	The dress is too long for her.
Was Sie gesagt haben, ist uns nicht ganz klar.	What you have said is not quite clear to us.
Die Aufgabe scheint ihm ganz leicht.	The lesson seems quite easy to (for) him.
Der Kopf tut mir weh.	I have a headache.

The following list includes some common adjectives that take the dative.

ähnlich	like, similar (to)	**lieb**	dear
angenehm	pleasant	**möglich**	possible (for)
bekannt	known, familiar	**nützlich**	useful (to)
bequem	comfortable	**recht**	(all) right,
böse	angry (with)		agreeable (to)
dankbar	grateful (to)	**schwer**	difficult (for)
feindlich	hostile (toward)	**treu**	faithful (to)
fremd	strange (to)	**verwandt**	related (to)
freundlich	friendly, kind (to)	**weh**	painful, sad
gleich	equal, similar (to)	**wichtig**	important
leicht	easy (for)		(to)
leid: es tut mir leid I am sorry		**willkommen**	welcome (to)

103) Dative of Interest

The person interested in, or affected by, an entire statement is indicated by the dative form.

Du kommst mir gerade recht.   You're coming at just the right time, I would say.

104) Verbs with Genitive Complements

Genitive complements of verbs are rare in modern usage, but they are found in literature. The following list includes the commonest of these.

anklagen	accuse of
sich bedienen	use (make use of, avail oneself of)
bedürfen	need, have need of
sich bemächtigen	take possession of
beschuldigen	accuse of
sich erinnern (*also with* **an** + *acc.*)	remember
sich freuen (*also with* **über** + *acc.*)	be glad of
gedenken	remember, think of
sich rühmen	boast of
sich schämen (*also with* **wegen**)	be ashamed of

105) Adjectives with Genitive Complements

The following adjectives follow their genitive complements. *Example:* **Sind Sie der Sache gewiß?** *Are you sure of the matter?*

bedürftig	needy, in need of	**mächtig (sein)**	have mastery of
bewußt	aware (of)	**müde**	tired (of)
fähig (*also* **zu**)	capable of	**sicher**	sure, safe
froh (*also* **über**)	glad (of)	**verdächtig**	suspected (of)
gewiß	sure, certain (of)	**würdig**	worthy (of)

The directional meanings precede their complements.

nördlich (*also* **von**)	north (of)	**südlich** (*also* **von**)	south (of)
östlich " "	east (of)	**westlich** " "	west (of)

106) Genitive for Description

The genitive form often describes or modifies.

Fahren Sie erster Klasse?	Are you traveling first class?
Alle waren guter Laune.	All were in a good mood.
Sind Sie derselben Meinung wie ich?	Are you of the same opinion as I am?

107) Accusative with **los, gewohnt, lang,** and **entlang**

Ich möchte das schwere Gepäck los sein (werden).	I would like to be rid of (get rid of) the heavy baggage.
Sind Sie diese Arbeit schon gewohnt?	Are you accustomed to this work already?
Er bleibt einen Monat lang in der Stadt.	He is staying in the city for a month.
Jeden Morgen gehe ich den Park entlang.	Every morning I walk along the park.

ORAL EXERCISE

Complete the German sentences.

1. Ich bin (   ) nicht gewiß. (*his name, your address*)

2. Bedienen Sie sich (   ). (*a sharp knife*)

3. Wir sind (   ) gefolgt. (*those people*)

4. Die Polizei bemächtigte sich (   ). (*the stolen car*)

5. Man klagte den Mann (   ) an. (*stealing*)

6. Wie gefällt (   ) dieser Film? (*you, him, her, them*)

7. Diese Bücher gehören (   ). (*me, you, them*)

8. Dieses Gedicht ist (   ) unbekannt. (*the class, the teacher*)

9. Jetzt schämte er sich (   ). (*his foolishness*)

10. Fast niemand fährt (   ). (*third class*)

11. Der Diener gehorcht (   ). (*his master*)

12. Die Mädchen schmeicheln (   ). (*their father, their aunt, their parents*)

13. Bedürfen Sie (   )? (*my help*)

14. Diese Fragen sind (   ) nicht zu schwer. (*for our students*)

15. Der Junge sieht (   ) ähnlich. (*his father, his sister*)

16. Das ist (   ) nicht ganz klar. (*us, them, the teacher*)

17. Wer ist (   ) müde? (*working*)

18. Ich muß (   ) das Gesicht waschen. (*the baby*)

19. Viele Leute sind (   ) entlaufen. (*the Eastern Zone*)

20. Die Flucht gelang (   ). (*the young man, the old people*)

WRITTEN EXERCISE

1. It seems to me that children often become tired of playing.

2. Would you advise me (as to) whether I should use a dictionary in this course?

3. If those stories are too easy for you, you will like these novels. (*gefallen*)

4. I want to congratulate you on your new position.

5. It has just occurred to me that this question resembles the first one.

6. Although there is no dative in English, one soon succeeds in using the forms correctly in German.

7. South of the Alps the climate is much warmer than in Germany.

8. In the city I met your brother, who resembles you very much.

9. If you were not sure of the assignment, you should have asked the teacher.

10. When the general commands the soldiers to do something, they always obey him.

11. This chair is not comfortable for me because it hurts my back.

12. Do you know which coat belongs to the speaker?

13. Take the hammer away from the baby so that he doesn't hurt himself.

14. Do not boast too much of your good luck.

15. If the dress did not fit the little girl, she could not wear it.

16. A thief stole the car from my neighbor and then escaped from the police.

17. My sister did not succeed in reading the entire book.

18. Many people wanted to congratulate the young poet on his new book.

19. The rain was welcome to the farmers because they needed a big harvest.

20. If you wanted to get rid of the insects, you could use poison. (*sich bedienen*)

LESSON 13

RELATIVE PRONOUNS

108) Relative Pronouns in English

In English a relative pronoun introduces a subordinate clause. Its case depends on its use in its own clause.

The students *who* have not bought books must do so immediately.
The students *whose* books have not arrived will have an assignment in the library.
The students to *whom* the professor was talking have gone to the library.
The students *whom* we saw yesterday were studying German.

109) Relative Pronouns in German

German has two relative pronouns, **der** and **welcher,** which are interchangeable except that **welcher** has no genitive forms. **Der** is more common than **welcher.**

	der				welcher			
	M.	F.	N.	Pl.	M.	F.	N.	Pl.
N.	der	die	das	die	welcher	welche	welches	welche
G.	dessen	deren	dessen	deren	—	—	—	—
D.	dem	der	dem	denen	welchem	welcher	welchem	welchen
A.	den	die	das	die	welchen	welche	welches	welche

The relative pronoun must agree in gender and number with its antecedent, but its case is determined by its use in its own clause. The relative pronoun is never omitted in German.

Der Student, der (welcher) **Die Studentin, die (welche)** } **keine Bücher** **gekauft hat, muß es jetzt tun.**	The student who has not bought books must do so now.
Ein Student, dessen Bücher **Eine Studentin, deren Bücher** } **hier sind,** **darf jetzt lesen.**	A student whose books are here may read now.
Die Studenten, denen (welchen) **der Professor Bücher geliehen** **hat, dürfen sie bis Montag be-** **halten.**	The students to whom the professor lent books may keep them until Monday.
Die Studenten, die (welche) wir **noch nicht kennen, werden bald** **hier sein.**	The students (whom) we don't know yet will soon be here.

110) wer and was

Sometimes there is no noun antecedent to determine the gender of the relative pronoun. Then the interrogatives **wer** and **was** serve as relatives to distinguish between people and things. **Wer** and **was** are frequently followed by a demonstrative pronoun in the next clause.

N.	**wer**	**was**
G.	**wessen**	—
D.	**wem**	—
A.	**wen**	**was**

Wer das getan hat, (der) versteht **seine Sache.**	Whoever did that knows his business.
Was das bedeutet, (das) weiß **niemand.**	What that means nobody knows.
Wessen Buch das ist, (das) weiß ich **nicht.**	Whose book that is I don't know.

When the antecedent is a clause or a neuter substantive other than a noun, the relative pronoun is **was.** The neuter substantives include **alles, etwas, nichts, vieles, manches,** and neuter abstractions formed from adjectives (**das Gute, das Beste**).

Es ist nicht alles Gold, was glänzt.	Not everything that glitters is gold.
Das war das Schlimmste, was ihm hätte geschehen können.	That was the worst thing that could have happened to him.
Er erzählte uns eine lustige Geschichte, was uns sehr erfreute.	He told us an amusing story, (an event) which pleased us greatly.

(**Was** indicates that the antecedent is the entire clause, not **Geschichte.**)

111) wo– and wor–

Wo– or **wor–** may replace the forms of **der, welcher** and **was** in combination with prepositions governing the dative or accusative case, provided the antecedent is not a person.

Die Länder, wovon (von welchen, von denen) er sprach, hatte er viel bereist.	He had traveled a great deal through the lands that he talked about.
Er hatte die Stadt nicht gern, worin (in welcher, in der) er lange gelebt hatte.	He didn't like the city in which he had lived for a long time.
Ich verstehe nichts, worüber er spricht.	I don't understand anything that he is talking about.
Ich kenne den Mann, über den (welchen) er spricht.	I know the man (whom, that) he is talking about.

ORAL EXERCISE

Translate.

1. Whose parents did you see there?

2. For whom are you waiting?

3. The pencil with which I write is red.

4. Tell us all you know about him.

5. Who is the man whom you see there?

6. What is the matter with them?

7. Of whom are you thinking?

8. My daughter, whose picture you see, is not here.

9. I understood nothing he said.

10. The lake on which I live is small.

11. Many a thing he did was good.

12. The boy who has just walked out speaks German.

13. The child with whom he was playing began to cry.

14. This is the best I can do.

15. Do you know whose house that is?

16. He who has no friend is poor.

17. Of what are you thinking?

18. I bought the best he had.

19. All those with whom I was working have left.

20. The letters you have in your hand are from my sister.

WRITTEN EXERCISE

1. The woman whose son was in my class has gone to the country.

2. The gentlemen with whom I spoke this morning live in a small village on the Rhine.

3. I told him I was well again, which surprised him.

4. The teacher whom you saw just now said something in class this morning which I did not understand.

5. The street on which his car was stolen was very dark.

6. The pencil that I found belongs to my friend's father.

7. The students look forward to the vacation which they have during the summer.

8. Whoever says that doesn't know anything about music.

9. I do not exactly remember what happened after the accident.

10. The train on which he arrived two weeks ago was forty minutes late.

11. Students whose parents are rich drive around in big cars and wear expensive clothes.

12. The man whose beautiful voice I admire sang the leading role in the opera last Sunday.

13. Good parents are interested in everything that their children do.

14. A little dog that ran across the street was almost hit by a car.

15. The book of which you are thinking contains an interesting story about life in a big city.

16. Little children to whom mothers tell fairy tales usually pay close (*scharf*) attention.

17. That is a means on which one can depend when one comes face to face with danger.

18. That is the most beautiful thing I have ever seen.

19. I have just read the book which our instructor recommended.

20. The teacher whose class I attended explained a poem which he had read to the students.

LESSON 14

COMPARISON OF ADJECTIVES
AND ADVERBS

112) Formation

When added to positive forms of adjectives and adverbs, **–er** and **–st** identify the comparative and superlative forms, respectively. The comparative form of an adjective ending in **–el** loses the **e** before **l** (**edel, edler**). Adjectives ending in **–en** or **–er** may drop or retain the **e**: **golden: goldener** or **goldner**; **teuer: teuerer** or **teurer**.

The superlative **–st** becomes **–est** after **d, t, s, st, ß, tz, x,** and **z**: **der heißeste Tag, der weiteste Weg.** The **e** is optional after **sch,** but it is not added after the participial **–end** and the suffix **–isch**.

POSITIVE	COMPARATIVE
klar clear	**klarer**
schwer heavy	**schwerer**
hold gracious	**holder**
interessant interesting	**interessanter**
teuer dear, expensive	**teu(e)rer**
reizend charming	**reizender**
komisch funny	**komischer**

ATTRIBUTIVE SUPERLATIVE	PREDICATE SUPERLATIVE
der klarste	am klarsten
der schwerste	am schwersten
der holdeste	am holdesten
der interessanteste	am interessantesten
der teuerste	am teuersten
der reizendste	am reizendsten
der komischste	am komischsten

113) Umlaut in Comparative and Superlative

The following monosyllabic adjectives have umlauted vowels in their comparative and superlative forms.

alt old	älter	der älteste	am ältesten
arg bad, severe	ärger	der ärgste	am ärgsten
arm poor	ärmer	der ärmste	am ärmsten
dumm stupid	dümmer	der dümmste	am dümmsten
grob coarse, rude	gröber	der gröbste	am gröbsten
groß big, great, tall	größer	der größte	am größten
hart harsh, severe	härter	der härteste	am härtesten
hoch high, tall	höher	der höchste	am höchsten
jung young	jünger	der jüngste	am jüngsten
kalt cold	kälter	der kälteste	am kältesten
klug clever	klüger	der klügste	am klügsten
krank sick	kränker	der kränkste	am kränksten
kurz short	kürzer	der kürzeste	am kürzesten
lang long	länger	der längste	am längsten
nah near, close	näher	der nächste	am nächsten
rot red	röter	der röteste	am rötesten
scharf sharp	schärfer	der schärfste	am schärfsten
schwach weak	schwächer	der schwächste	am schwächsten
schwarz black	schwärzer	der schwärzeste	am schwärzesten
stark strong	stärker	der stärkste	am stärksten
warm warm	wärmer	der wärmste	am wärmsten

114) A few monosyllabic adjectives form their comparative and superlative forms either with or without umlaut of the stem vowel: **naß, nasser (nässer), der nasseste (nässeste), am nassesten (nässesten).** This group includes the following:

blaß	pale	**naß**	wet
fromm	pious	**schmal**	narrow
gesund	well, healthy	**krumm**	crooked
glatt	smooth		

115) Irregular Forms

bald soon	**eher**		**am ehesten**
gern gladly	**lieber**		**am liebsten**
groß big, great	**größer**	**der größte**	**am größten**
gut good	**besser**	**der beste**	**am besten**
hoch high, tall	**höher**	**der höchste**	**am höchsten**
nah near, close	**näher**	**der nächste**	**am nächsten**
sehr very (much)	**mehr**		**am meisten**
viel much	**mehr**	**der meiste**	**am meisten**
wenig (a) little	**minder**	**der mindeste**	**am mindesten**
	(weniger)	**(der wenigste)**	**(am wenigsten)**
wohl well	**besser**		**am besten**

116) Usage

The comparative and superlative forms have uses corresponding to English usage. Adjective endings are added to the comparative and superlative forms when they are used attributively. An article always precedes a superlative attributive adjective.

Der Junge will den größeren Apfel haben.	The boy wants (to have) the larger apple.
Der Junge will den größten Apfel haben.	The boy wants the largest apple.
Welcher Apfel ist größer?	Which apple is larger?
Welcher Apfel ist der größte von allen?	Which apple is the largest of all?
Die meisten Leute wollen längere Ferien.	Most people want longer vacations.

117) Forms in the Predicate

The predicate adjective and adverb are not distinguished from each other in form. This is true of the comparative and superlative forms also. For this reason, the **am**-form of the superlative is used both as a predicate adjective and as an adverb. When a superlative adverbial modifier is required, the **am**-form is necessary.

Diese Dame ist schön.	This lady is beautiful.
Diese Dame singt schön.	This lady sings beautifully.
Diese Dame ist schöner als ihre Schwester.	This lady is more beautiful than her sister.
Diese Dame singt schöner als ihre Schwester.	This lady sings more beautifully than her sister.
Diese Dame ist die schönste der drei Schwestern.	This lady is the most beautiful of the three sisters.
Diese Dame singt am schönsten.	This lady sings most beautifully (of all).

Sometimes the logical meaning makes the adjectival form impossible after **sein.**

Die Kartoffeln sind im Frühling am teuersten.	Potatoes are most expensive in the spring. (*No comparison is being made between some potatoes and others.*)

118) The Absolute Comparative and Superlative

The comparative form frequently qualifies the meaning of the adjective, although no direct comparison is made.

eine ältere Dame	a comparatively old lady, an elderly lady
die neueren Sprachen	modern languages
eine längere Reise	a rather long trip

A special superlative form with **aufs** describes a high degree of meaning, although no direct comparison is made.

Die Dame singt aufs schönste.	The lady sings most beautifully (as beautifully as can be expected).

119) höchst and äußerst

The superlative forms **höchst** and **äußerst** express a high degree and are synonymous with **sehr, recht, überaus, durch und durch,** and **durchaus.**

Das ist ein höchst (äußerst) interes-   That is a most interesting (extremely
santer Roman.   interesting) novel.

120) Special Patterns

The following word patterns must be learned as combinations.

so ... wie	**Der Vater ist nicht so groß wie der Sohn.**
	The father is not as tall as the son.
... –er als	**Der Sohn ist größer als der Vater.**
	The son is taller than the father.
je ... desto	**Je mehr man studiert, desto mehr weiß man.**
	The more you study, the more you know.
immer ... –er	**Der Kranke fühlt sich immer besser.**
	The patient is feeling better and better.
eher ... als	**Wir sind manchmal eher faul als müde**
(mehr ... als)	**(mehr faul als müde).**
	Sometimes we are more lazy than tired.

121) Superlative Adverbs

The following special forms are used adverbially.

bestens	as well as possible
frühestens	as early as possible, at the earliest, not before
höchstens	at most, at best
meistens	usually, mostly, as a rule
möglichst (bald, etc.)	as (soon) as possible
spätestens	at the latest
wenigstens	at least

ORAL EXERCISES

A. *Compare the following adjectives.*

1. arm
2. dichterisch
3. fremd
4. hoch
5. kompliziert

6. lieb
7. nah
8. überraschend
9. verständlich
10. wichtig

B. *Decline in singular and plural the German equivalent of:*

1. his younger son
2. the largest city
3. our oldest book
4. a more significant answer (use *bedeutend*)
5. the most complex airplane

⅚ WRITTEN EXERCISE

✓ 1. My friend is a fast runner, but my brother is the fastest runner of us all.
2. Most workers drive to the factories at six or seven o'clock in the morning.
3. If the larger birds flew faster than the smaller ones, the ostrich should fly fastest.
4. After the cold weather, many plants seemed more dead than alive.
5. The older my father gets, the less he reads.
✓ 6. That was an exceedingly stupid question you asked the doctor.
7. Because we did not start earlier, it will be at least midnight before we finish our sentences.
✓ 8. The pear tree is taller than the cherry tree, but just as tall as the apple tree.
9. The elderly lady could still sing most beautifully.

10. The weather got worse and worse and we decided we would rather stay home.

11. If I had studied harder, I would have been the most intelligent student in the class.

~12. On the next day he took a rather long walk through the woods.

13. He just told me a short story which impressed me most deeply.

14. The elderly stranger asked if it was always hottest here in July.

15. The farther we drove into the country, the more beautiful the view was.

16. What I like least about (an) this house is that the rooms are extremely small.

√17. My knife is much better and sharper than yours.

18. A week ago, I drank a better wine in this inn; at least it was a better wine than this one.

19. There are people who prefer spring to fall, but I like summer best.

20. Most older students study much harder than the younger ones, but those who are preparing for a test study the hardest.

LESSON 15

PASSIVE VOICE

---

122) Formation

Passive verb forms are obtained by combining the appropriate tense of **werden** with the participle of the verb supplying the meaning. There are two passive infinitives, just as there are two active ones.

sehen to see	**gesehen werden** to be seen
gesehen haben to have seen	**gesehen worden sein** to have been seen

Synopsis, Indicative Active	Synopsis, Indicative Passive
Der Mann schreibt den Brief.	**Der Brief wird von dem Mann geschrieben.**
The man writes the letter.	The letter is (being) written by the man.
Der Mann schrieb den Brief.	**Der Brief wurde von dem Mann geschrieben.**
The man wrote the letter.	The letter was written by the man.
Der Mann hat den Brief geschrieben.	**Der Brief ist von dem Mann geschrieben worden.**
The man wrote (has written) the letter.	The letter was written (has been written) by the man.

Der Mann hatte den Brief geschrieben.

The man had written the letter.

Der Brief war von dem Mann
geschrieben worden.

The letter had been written by the
man.

Der Mann wird den Brief schreiben.

The man will write the letter.

Der Brief wird von dem Mann
geschrieben werden.

The letter will be written by the
man.

Der Mann wird den Brief geschrieben haben.

The man will have written the
letter.

Der Brief wird von dem Mann
geschrieben worden sein.

The letter will have been written
by the man.

Indirect Discourse

Die Frau sagte, der Brief werde (or
würde) von ihrem Mann ge-
schrieben.

The woman said the letter was being
written by her husband.

Die Frau sagte, der Brief sei (or
wäre) von ihrem Mann ge-
schrieben worden.

The woman said the letter had been
written by her husband.

Die Frau sagte, der Brief werde (or
würde) von ihrem Mann ge-
schrieben werden.

The woman said the letter would be
written by her husband.

Die Frau sagte, der Brief werde (or
würde) von ihrem Mann ge-
schrieben worden sein.

The woman said the letter would
have been written by her husband.

123) Indirect Object

The indirect object of an active verb form can never become the subject
of a passive verb form, as in the English *He was given a reward*. The German
indirect object occurs in the dative case with both active and passive verb
forms. Some intransitive verbs also have passive forms with an impersonal
subject, which is not necessarily stated.

Eine Belohnung wurde ihm gege-
ben.

A reward was given to him (He was
given a reward).

Man hilft immer einem Un-glücklichen.	
Es wird einem Unglücklichen immer geholfen.	An unfortunate person is always helped.
Einem Unglücklichen wird im-mer geholfen.	

Ihm wurde alles geglaubt.	Everything he said was believed (He was believed in everything).

124) Prepositions with the Passive Voice

A. **Von** indicates agency of a person or an animal, sometimes of a thing.

Der Dieb ist von dem Schutzmann gesehen worden.	The thief was seen by the policeman.
Der Vogel ist von der Katze ge-fangen worden.	The bird was caught by the cat.
Der Ast wurde vom Wind abge-brochen.	The limb was broken off by the wind.

B. **Durch** indicates means, either of a person or of a thing.

Durch Friedrich den Großen wurde Preußen zu einer Welt-macht.	Prussia was developed into a world power by Frederick the Great. (**Durch** suggests *through the efforts of*, while **von** implies performance of a specific action by a person.)
Der Gefangene wurde durch seine Freunde befreit.	The prisoner was liberated by his friends. (He was released *through* or *because of* the friends' efforts.)
Viele Kranke werden durch die neuere Medizin geheilt.	Many sick people are cured by (means of) modern medical science.

C. **Mit** indicates the instrument of an action.

Seine Briefe werden immer mit der Schreibmaschine geschrie-ben.	His letters are always written on a a typewriter.
Die Suppe wird mit einem Löffel gegessen.	Soup is eaten with a spoon.

125) The Impersonal Passive

To describe a verbal action without naming the persons involved in the action, a passive form may be used with the impersonal **es** as a subject.

Es wurde getanzt = Man tanzte.	There was dancing.
Bis Mitternacht wurde getanzt.	Dancing went on until midnight.
Es wurde laut gelacht.	There was loud laughter.

126) Stylistic Substitutions for Passive Forms

A. **Man ißt die Suppe immer mit einem Löffel.**
One always eats soup (Soup is always eaten) with a spoon.

B. **Man öffnet die Tür um acht Uhr.**
Die Tür öffnet sich um acht Uhr.
The door is opened (opens) at eight o'clock.

C. **Es läßt sich leicht verstehen.**   It can easily be understood.
Das läßt sich nicht machen.   That can't be done.
Er läßt sich nicht sehen.   He won't see anybody.

D. **Das ist nicht zu machen.**   That can't be done.

ORAL EXERCISES

A. *Conjugate* rufen *in the six tenses of the indicative mood, passive voice.*

B. *Conjugate* sehen *in the eight forms of the subjunctive mood, passive voice.*

C. *Give a synopsis of*

1. verstehen *in the first person singular, indicative mood, passive voice.*

2. fortfahren *in the second person singular, subjunctive mood, passive voice.*

3. suchen *in the third person singular, subjunctive mood, passive voice.*

4. waschen *in the first person plural, indicative mood, passive voice.*

5. mitnehmen *in the second person plural, subjunctive mood, passive voice.*

6. finden *in the third person plural, indicative mood, passive voice.*

D. *Translate.*

1. I was asked for a cigarette.
2. He will be called every day.
3. They were brought home yesterday.
4. This kind of bread is baked every day.
5. He had been shot with a pistol.
6. I was given a new pen.
7. Many beautiful poems have been written.
8. The new words must be learned immediately.
9. The soldier was killed by a bullet.
10. Shoes are sold cheap here.

WRITTEN EXERCISE

1. Our new car, which had been stolen a week ago, was found by the police.
2. Grammatical errors are found in many a German theme.
3. We were told that this matter had been reported to you in the last letter.
4. People who cannot be advised cannot be helped.
5. The injured man was helped by a doctor who drove up right after the accident.
6. I was told that a prince had had this castle built in the twelfth century.
7. The most difficult exercises will often be written without mistakes by the best students.
8. The driver said the trip was not to be started in this weather.
9. It is to be expected that more houses will soon be built on this street.
10. I went to the store late in the afternoon and almost everything was already sold out.
11. At the party there was eating, drinking, and smoking the whole evening.
12. If one word had not been misspelled, the theme would have received the first prize.

13. The view from the top of the mountain cannot be described.

√14. These beautiful poems were written by a famous poet fifty years ago.

15. The dog was beaten with a stick because it did not obey its master.

16. It can be imagined that one doesn't like to translate such difficult sentences.

√17. The salesman said that the house was heated by a gas furnace.

18. After my sister had set the table, she said, "What is to be done now?"

19. That is not done in the United States, although it is done in some countries.

20. The robber would have been killed by the shot if he had taken another step.

LESSON 16

INFINITIVES AND PARTICIPLES

127) Infinitives as **das**-nouns

The infinitive used as a noun represents the action of the verb. It is neuter and is usually written with the article. It can be combined with modifiers into a single word.

Auf Lachen folgt Weinen.	Weeping follows laughter (laughing).
Das Rechnen kommt ihm schwer.	Figuring (arithmetic) is difficult for him.
Sein oder Nichtsein, das ist hier die Frage.	To be or not to be, that is the question.

128) Infinitives as Imperatives

The infinitive can express a brusque command or a public announcement.

Einsteigen!	All aboard!
Nicht rauchen!	No smoking (Do not smoke).

129) Infinitives as Modifiers

The active infinitive with **zu** serves as a predicate modifier after the verbs **sein, scheinen,** and **bleiben.** It also can modify direct objects.

Wo ist ein gutes Restaurant zu finden?	Where is a good restaurant to be found? (Where can a good restaurant be found)?
Wem nicht zu raten ist, dem ist auch nicht zu helfen.	Whoever cannot be advised cannot be helped either.
Das scheint ihm nicht zu gefallen.	He doesn't seem to like that.
Was bleibt noch zu tun?	What still remains to be done?
Wir haben noch viel zu tun.	We still have much to do.

130) The Gerundive

When the modifying infinitive with **zu** is moved to an attributive position, a special form called the gerundive is produced by adding **–d** and an adjective ending. Modifiers of the gerundive precede it.

Welche Bäume sind zu fällen? Die zu fällenden Bäume stehen jenseits des Hügels.	Which trees are to be felled? The trees to be felled are on the other side of the hill.
Allmählich zu leistende Zahlungen sind nicht immer so leicht, wie man sie sich vorstellt.	Time payments (payments to be made gradually) are not always as easy as one imagines them.

131) The Infinitive Clause with **zu**

The infinitive, by itself or combined with other elements to form an infinitive clause, may be a subject, a predicate complement, or an appositive. The infinitive clause is always set off by commas.

Es war unmöglich, ihn zu retten. **Ihn zu retten, war unmöglich.**	It was impossible to rescue him.
Die Aufgabe für morgen ist, eine neue Geschichte zu lesen.	Tomorrow's lesson is to read a new story.
Unsere Nachbarn haben die Absicht, nach Afrika zu reisen.	Our neighbors intend to travel (have the intention of traveling) to Africa.
Der Anstreicher hat versprochen, die Arbeit morgen früh anzufangen.	The painter has promised to begin work tomorrow morning.

132) The Infinitive with **zu** as Object of a Preposition

Three prepositions, **anstatt** *instead of*, **ohne** *without*, and **um** *in order to*, take the infinitive with **zu** as an object.

Ich machte einen Spaziergang, anstatt hier zu bleiben.	I took a walk instead of staying here.

133) The Present Participle

The present participle is formed by adding **–d** to the infinitive.

Exceptions: **seiend, tuend.** It is used adjectivally or adverbially.

Sein letzter Aufsatz ist hervorragend.	His last theme is outstanding.
Er hat einen hervorragenden Aufsatz geschrieben.	He wrote an outstanding theme.
Sie grüßte ihn lächelnd.	She greeted him with a smile.

134) Present Participles as Nouns

When a present participle is used as a noun, it is capitalized and has a declensional ending.

der Reisende	the traveler (*masc.*)	**ein Reisender**	a traveler (*masc.*)
die Reisende	the traveler (*fem.*)	**eine Reisende**	a traveler (*fem.*)
die Reisenden	the travelers		

135) Perfect Participles as Modifiers

The perfect participle is commonly used either as an attributive adjective or as a predicate adjective. **Kommen** is commonly modified by the perfect participle of an intransitive verb.

Ein längst vergessener Maler wird zuweilen wiederentdeckt.	A long forgotten painter is sometimes rediscovered.
Meine Aufgabe ist noch nicht gemacht.*	My lesson is not yet done.
Der kleine Junge kam gelaufen.	The little boy came running.

* Note that the adjectival use of the participle must be distinguished from the use of the participle with the passive voice, the latter indicating that an action is being performed.

136) Perfect Participles as Imperatives

By itself, the perfect participle expresses a sharp command or warning.

Aufgestanden!	Get (Stand) up!
Aufgepasst!	Look out!

137) Perfect Participles as Nouns

When a perfect participle is used as a noun, it has a capital letter and a declensional ending.

der Bekannte	the acquaintance (*masc.*)	**ein Bekannter**	an acquaintance (*masc.*)
die Bekannte	the acquaintance (*fem.*)	**eine Bekannte**	an acquaintance (*fem.*)
die Bekannten	the acquaintances		

138) The Extended Adjectival Modifier

The extended adjectival (or participial) modifier occurs in both English and German. Its elements always appear in the same sequence: article, adverb, adjective, noun.

Example: a not very popular but unusually well-written novel

Study the arrangement of the German examples.*

Das noch nicht lange gebräuchliche Mittel heißt, wenn ich nicht irre, Pentathol.	The anesthetic, (which has as) yet not (been) long in use, is called pentathol, if I am not mistaken.
... **Biographie des teuren, vom Schicksal so furchtbar heimgesuchten, erhobenen und gestürzten Mannes ...**	... biography of the dear man (who was) so terribly afflicted, exalted and destroyed by fate ...

If the adjective is the present participle of a transitive verb, an object precedes it.

... **die immer stärker ihr Haupt erhebende Résistance ...**	... the Resistance, raising its head more and more forcefully ...

* These examples are quoted from Thomas Mann, the second from his *Dr. Faustus* and the other three from *Die Entstehung des Dr. Faustus*.

Dative relationships stand in the adverbial position.

Die Sommerwochen, in denen ich an den der Ubersiedelung Adrians nach München vorangehenden Kápiteln schrieb, brachten uns einen mir wichtigen Besuch.	The summer weeks, during which I was writing on the chapters preceding Adrian's moving to Munich, brought us a visit (which was) important to me.

ORAL EXERCISES

A. *Eliminate the relative clauses.*

    Example: Ich sehe einen Jungen, der im Garten spielt.

           Ich sehe einen im Garten spielenden Jungen.

1. Das Holz, das am Strande liegt, kann man verbrennen.
2. Das Holz, das man am Strande findet, kann man verbrennen.
3. Der Dichter hat zwei Romane geschrieben, die noch nicht veröffentlicht worden sind.
4. Ein Student, der schnell liest, kann vieles lernen.
5. Die Bücher, die in Fraktur gedruckt worden sind, gefallen den meisten Studenten nicht.

B. *Translate.*

1. We have much to do today.
2. It is to be hoped that we can do everything.
3. Swimming and walking are good for us.
4. "Stand up," said the teacher.
5. It is not always easy to remember names.

WRITTEN EXERCISE

1. According to some doctors, too much smoking is injurious to many people.

2. It is time to go downtown and meet my friends.

3. Without looking around, the guide said, "Walk to the left." (*Express the imperative in as many different ways as possible.*)

4. All sentences to be written are to be found at the end of each lesson.

5. I had helped my brother study German three days before the test.

6. The stories to be read tomorrow have been written by great scholars of the last century.

7. Instead of studying diligently and attending lectures, some students waste too much time.

8. Scientists have said that it will be possible to fly to the moon sometime.

9. Each one of the employees is said to have worked for this company longer than twenty-five years.

10. At the end of the day, the farmer said he was tired of working.

11. Did you see the books (that were) placed on your desk?

12. Across the street stands a house to be sold.

13. Pencils are not to be used without the teacher's having permitted it.

14. The men to be honored today performed never-to-be-forgotten deeds during the last war.

15. All men serving in the last war were allowed to go to the university without paying tuition.

16. The barefoot boy came running across the yard and cut his foot on the broken bottle.

17. If the official had given the travelers better advice, their passports would have been examined faster.

18. Children go to school to get a good education and to prepare themselves better for life.

19. To be successful is a goal toward which all people should strive.

20. We had decided to spend the weekend at the lake, but we stayed at home because it began to rain.

LESSON 17

NUMERALS AND
TIME EXPRESSIONS

139) Forms

CARDINALS		ORDINALS		FRACTIONS
0	null			
1	eins	der, die, das erste	1/2	ein halb; die Hälfte
2	zwei	der zweite	1-1/2	eineinhalb; anderthalb
3	drei	der dritte	1/3	das Drittel
4	vier	der vierte	1/4	das Viertel
5	fünf	der fünfte	1/5	das Fünftel
6	sechs	der sechste	1/6	das Sechstel
7	sieben	der sieb(en)te	1/7	das Sieb(en)tel
8	acht	der achte	1/8	das Achtel
9	neun	der neunte	1/9	das Neuntel
10	zehn	der zehnte	1/10	das Zehntel
11	elf		1/11	
12	zwölf		1/12	
13	dreizehn		1/13	
14	vierzehn		1/14	
15	fünfzehn	–te	1/15	–tel
16	sechzehn		1/16	
17	siebzehn		1/17	
18	achtzehn		1/18	
19	neunzehn		1/19	

CARDINALS	ORDINALS		FRACTIONS
20 zwanzig	der zwanzigste	1/20	das Zwanzigstel
21 einundzwanzig		1/21	
30 dreißig		1/30	
40 vierzig		1/40	
50 fünfzig		1/50	
60 sechzig	–ste	1/60	–stel
70 siebzig		1/70	
80 achtzig		1/80	
90 neunzig		1/90	
100 hundert		1/100	
101 hunderteins	der hunderterste	1/101	das Hunderteintel
102 hundertzwei	der hundertzweite	1/102	das Hundertzweitel
121 hunderteinund-	der hunderteinund-	1/121	das Hunderteinund-
zwanzig	zwanzigste		zwanzigstel
200 zweihundert	der zweihundertste	1/200	das Zweihundertstel
1000 tausend	der tausendste	1/1000	das Tausendstel

Values from *million* are nouns.

1 000 000 **eine Million**	2 000 000 000 **zwei Milliarden**
2 000 000 **zwei Millionen**	1 000 000 000 000 **eine Billion**
1 000 000 000 **eine Milliarde**	2 000 000 000 000 **zwei Billionen**

140) Cardinal Numbers

Eins is indeclinable when used abstractly. When it stands before a noun, it is declined like the indefinite article **ein.** The other cardinal numbers are indeclinable.

141) Derivatives of Cardinals

Derivatives are formed from cardinals by adding certain suffixes.

–er: indeclinable adjective

in den vierziger Jahren des letz-   in the forties of the last century
ten Jahrhunderts

–erlei: indeclinable adjective

zweierlei   two kinds of
dreierlei   three kinds of

–fach: adjective or adverb

einfach	simple, simply
zweifach	double, twofold
dreifach	triple, threefold

–mal: adverb

einmal	once
zweimal	twice
dreimal	three times

–malig: adjective

einmalig	happening but once, unique
zweimalig	happening twice, repeated
dreimalig	occurring three times

142) im Jahre

A year is designated by a cardinal number with or without the phrase **im Jahre.**

Amerika wurde (im Jahre) 1492 entdeckt. America was discovered in 1492.

143) Ordinal Numbers

The ordinal numbers are adjectives with declensional endings. They are formed by adding **–t** to the cardinals from **zwei** to **neunzehn** and **–st** to the cardinals from **zwanzig** to **hundert.** Exceptions are **der erste,** *the first*; **der dritte,** *the third*; **der achte,** *the eighth*.

Der fünfte Monat heißt Mai.   The fifth month is called May.

Calendar dates are ordinals modifying the name of the month, which is always masculine.

Der wievielte ist heute?   What date (day of the month) is
Den wievielten haben wir heute?   today?

Heute ist der achtzehnte (18.) Juli.	Today is the eighteenth of July.
Heute haben wir den achtzehnten (18.) Juli.	

Weihnachten fällt auf den fünfundzwanzigsten (25.) Dezember.	Christmas falls on the twenty-fifth of December.
Wer wurde am zweiundzwanzigsten (22.) Februar geboren?	Who was born on February 22nd?

144) Ordinal Adverbs

Ordinal adverbs are formed by adding **–ens** to the ordinal stem.

erstens	first, in the first place
zweitens	second, in the second place
drittens	third, in the third place

145) Fractions

The numerator of a fraction is a cardinal number. The denominator is a **das**-noun formed by adding **–el** to the stem of the ordinal.

Er hat drei Viertel des Weins getrunken.	He drank three fourths of the wine.

Exception: one half is **die Hälfte;** the adjective form is **halb.**

Die Mutter gab dem Kind die Hälfte eines Apfels (einen halben Apfel).	The mother gave the child half an apple.
Nur die Hälfte der Arbeit wurde gemacht.	Only half of the work was done.

146) Arithmetical Terminology

+	**und, plus**	**4 und (plus) 3 ist 7**
−	**weniger, minus**	**9 weniger (minus) 3 ist 6**
✕, ·	**mal**	**4 mal 4 ist 16**
:	**(geteilt) durch**	**12 (geteilt) durch 4 ist 3**
=	**ist, gleich**	

147) Decimals

In German the decimal is indicated by a comma.

2.75 = 2,75 **zwei Komma sieben fünf** *or* **zwei und fünfundsiebzig Hundertstel.**

148) Time by the Clock

Wieviel Uhr ist es?	
Wieviel ist die Uhr?	What time is it?
Wie spät ist es?	
Es ist drei (Uhr).	It is three (o'clock).
Es ist zehn Minuten vor (bis) acht.	It is ten minutes to eight.
Es ist zehn Minuten nach acht.	It is ten minutes after eight.
Es ist Viertel nach vier.	
Es ist Viertel fünf.	It is a quarter after four (4:15).
Es ist vier Uhr fünfzehn.	
Es ist halb fünf.	It is half past four (4:30).
Es ist vier Uhr dreißig.	
Es ist Viertel vor fünf.	
Es ist drei Viertel fünf.	It is a quarter to five (4:45).
Es ist vier Uhr fünfundvierzig.	
Die Klasse beginnt um acht (Uhr).	Class starts at eight (o'clock).

Europeans use the twenty-four hour system more than Americans do. The day begins at **0.00 Uhr (null Uhr)** and ends at **24.00 Uhr.** This system is used in timetables and public affairs schedules. *3:30* P.M. is **15.30 (15 Uhr 30)** on such schedules.

ORAL EXERCISES

A. *Read in German.*

9	66	202	704
13	71	296	893
22	87	321	999
30	88	377	1000
33	95	418	1492
44	101	598	8639
52	173	625	1 345 892

Gestern war der 4., 7., 13., 20., 23., 30., Juli.

B. *Read in German.*

$3 + 6 = 9$	$21 - 6 = 15$	$25 \times 3 = 75$
$17 - 12 = 5$	$5 \times 6 = 30$	$85:5 = 17$
$7 \times 7 = 49$	$35:7 = 5$	$383 + 28 = 411$
$36:6 = 6$	$110 + 25 = 135$	$397 - 40 = 357$
$12 + 48 = 60$	$124 - 12 = 112$	$120 \times 4 = 480$

C. *Read in German.*

1/4	3/4	7/9	7/20	3/100
1/2	2/3	9/15	16/31	13/1000

D. *Read the following times of day in different ways in German.*

7.30	10.45	5.14	9.01
4.15	3.50	8.38	12.21

WRITTEN EXERCISE

1. The man in the second row was sitting next to two pretty ladies.
2. If today is the nineteenth of June, a week from today will be the twenty-sixth.
3. Which of the three sisters is interested in music?
4. The child had eaten half a roll and had drunk half a glass of milk.
5. Lessing, the third great German poet of the eighteenth century, was born in 1729.
6. There was a twofold reason why I didn't go: in the first place, I had no money, and, in the second place, it was raining.
7. Three eighths is one half of three fourths.
8. How many times have you heard Beethoven's Ninth Symphony?
9. On what day of the month will the first meeting be held?
10. The letter had been written on the eighteenth of January but had not been mailed until the twenty-first.
11. The movie started at 7:30 and was over at 9:45.
12. Thomas Mann, one of the greatest novelists of our century, was born in the seventies of the last century.
13. If you remember all these details, the professor will have the shock of his life.
14. On the first day after vacation one eighth of the class was absent.
15. The Zugspitze, Germany's highest mountain, is 9,641 feet high.
16. If the girl had paid attention during the explanation, she would not have had all kinds of difficulties with the sentences.
17. A man in his sixties helped many children cross the street every day.
18. The students acted as if Lesson Seventeen were the most difficult of all.
19. Thousands of people waste their time by playing cards.
20. We have had to translate twenty English sentences into German seventeen times.

APPENDIXES

WORD ORDER

Since the conjugated verb form (inflected or finite verb form) is the most important part of a sentence or clause, a definite position is assigned to it. From the position of the conjugated verb form, which may stand first, second, or last in a clause, we can determine with what kind of clause we are concerned.

The first principle of German word order is that the conjugated verb form is the second element of a sentence. The subject, with all its modifiers, may stand in the first or third position. Any syntactical unit of the sentence (object, adverb, adverbial phrase, or clause) may occupy the first position for emphasis or for stylistic reasons.

The second principle of German word order is that the respective arrangement of the units in the predicate depends on degree of emphasis. The final position gives greatest emphasis, and the position immediately after the verb (or subject, if third) is the least emphatic one. Therefore infinitives, participles, and separable prefixes, most significant to the completion of the verbal meaning, must stand last. The next most significant element is often the direct object or predicate adjective.

The third principle of German word order is that adjectives and adverbs precede the words or phrases they modify. When an adverb modifies the verb, it must stand last or as near the end as the verbal complements permit. A series of modifiers of the verb is arranged according to degree of emphasis.

When we speak of the three types of word order, normal, inverted, and transposed (or dependent), we are concerned with the position of the conjugated verb form.

Normal: **Er schreibt einen Brief.**⎫
Inverted: **Einen Brief schreibt er.**⎬ He is writing a letter.
Transposed: **Ich weiß, daß er einen**   I know that he is writing a letter.
            Brief schreibt.

A. Normal Word Order

1. The subject, with modifiers, stands first and is immediately followed by the verb.

Er schreibt einen Brief.   He is writing a letter.
Der junge Mann, der nicht liest,   The young man who is not reading is
  schreibt einen Brief.   writing a letter.

2. When a verb with a separable prefix is used in a simple tense, the prefix goes to the end of the clause.

Er steht um sieben Uhr auf.   He gets up at seven o'clock.

3. Co-ordinating conjunctions (**aber, allein, denn, oder, sondern,** and **und**) do not affect the position of the conjugated verb form.

Er schreibt einen Brief, aber ich   He is writing a letter but I am read-
  lese ein Buch.   ing a book.

4. The predicate may include objects, adverbs, and/or other elements which are essential to complete the meaning of the verb.

   a. Order of objects

      (1) The indirect object precedes the direct object unless the direct object is a personal pronoun.

Er gibt dem Mann ein Buch.   He gives the man a book.
Er gibt ihm ein Buch.   He gives him a book.
Er gibt es dem Mann.   He gives it to the man.
Er gibt es ihm.   He gives it to him.
Er gibt dem Mann etwas.   He gives the man something.
Er gibt ihm etwas.   He gives him something.

(2) The reflexive pronoun, like personal pronoun objects, follows the conjugated verb form; i.e., it occupies the position of least emphasis.

Er wäscht sich die Hände.	He is washing his hands.

b. Order of adverbs

(1) Adverbs of time precede all other adverbs. The order of adverbs of place, manner, and degree varies according to their relative importance in the group, the most important appearing last. Adverbs of time may precede noun objects.

Sie ist um zehn Uhr schnell aus dem Hause gegangen.	She went out of the house quickly at ten o'clock.
Ich werde morgen die Rechnung bezahlen.	I'll pay the bill tomorrow.

(2) The more general adverb usually precedes the more specific adverb.

Er geht heute um elf Uhr in die Deutschstunde.	He is going to the German class today at eleven o'clock.
Er sitzt im Zimmer am offenen Fenster.	He is sitting by the open window in the (his) room.
Er wohnt hier in der Stadt.	He is living here in the city.

c. Predicate complements

Predicate complements are the predicate noun, predicate adjective, adverb, separable prefix, perfect participle, and infinitive.

(1) Any one of the following four complements may stand at the end of an independent sentence.

Sie ist immer eine fleißige Studentin.	She is always a diligent student.
Sie wird jetzt sehr berühmt.	She is becoming very famous now.
Sie spielt wohl das Klavier gut.	She probably plays the piano well.
Sie bringt morgen ihren Freund mit.	She is bringing her friend along tomorrow.

(2) With the compound tenses, each of the four complements named in (1) precedes the perfect participle or the infinitive.

Sie ist immer eine fleißige Studentin gewesen.	She has always been a diligent student.
Sie wird immer eine fleißige Studentin sein.	She will always be a diligent student.
Sie ist im Ausland sehr berühmt geworden.	She has become very famous abroad.
Sie wird im Ausland sehr berühmt werden.	She will become very famous abroad.
Sie hat wohl das Klavier gut gespielt.	She has probably played the piano well.
Sie wird wohl das Klavier gut spielen.	She will probably play the piano well.
Sie hat gestern ihren Freund mitgebracht.	She brought her friend along yesterday.
Sie wird morgen ihren Freund mitbringen.	She will bring her friend along tomorrow.

d. Position of negative adverbs

(1) When a negative adverb modifies the verb, it stands at the end of the clause or just before the perfect participle, infinitive, or separable prefix.

Er studiert nicht.	He doesn't study.
Er studierte die Aufgabe nie.	He never studied the lesson.
Er wird morgen nicht kommen.	He won't come tomorrow.
Er hat mir gestern nicht geschrieben.	He didn't write to me yesterday.
Sie geht heute nicht mit.	She isn't going along today.

(2) When a negative adverb modifies a particular word or phrase, it precedes that word or phrase.

Sie ist nie eine berühmte Sängerin gewesen.	She has never been a famous singer.
Sie wird nie berühmt werden.	She will never become famous.
Sie hat die Lieder niemals gut gesungen.	She has never sung the songs well.
Dies ist nicht das richtige Buch.	This is not the right book.

Ich gehe nicht nach Hause, sondern in die Stadt.	I am not going home, but rather to town.
Ich trinke nie gern Bier.	I never like to drink beer.

B. Inverted Word Order

1. Whenever the sentence begins with an element other than the subject or a co-ordinating conjunction, the conjugated verb form precedes the subject.

Direct object: **Den Apfel gab er mir heute in der Schule.**

Indirect object: **Mir gab er heute den Apfel in der Schule.**

Adverb of place: **In der Schule gab er mir heute den Apfel.**

Adverb of time: **Heute gab er mir den Apfel in der Schule.**

He gave me an apple in school today.

Perfect Participle: **Gesehen habe ich den Mann.** — I have seen the man.

2. Questions also have inverted word order except when the subject is an interrogative pronoun or otherwise contains an interrogative form.

Hat er dir den Apfel in der Schule gegeben?	Did he give you the apple in school?
Wann sind Sie nach Hause gegangen?	When did you go home?
Was steht in dem Buch?	What is (written) in the book? (What does the book say?)
Welches Kind schreibt die Aufgabe?	Which child is writing the lesson?

3. When a complex sentence begins with a dependent clause, the independent clause has inverted word order.

Wenn Sie fleißiger studieren, werden Sie nicht durchfallen.	If you study harder, you will not fail.

C. Transposed Word Order

1. Subordinating conjunctions

Some of the most common subordinating conjunctions in German are **als, als ob, als wenn, bevor, da, damit, daß, ehe, nachdem, ob, seit**(dem), **während, weil,** and **wenn.**

    a. When a clause begins with a subordinating conjunction, the conjugated verb form stands at the end of the clause.

Er hat sich verspätet, weil er zu lange geschlafen hat.	He was late because he slept too long.
Er lief ins Haus, als er mich gestern sah.	He ran into the house when he saw me yesterday.
Als er mich gestern sah, lief er ins Haus.	When he saw me yesterday, he ran into the house.

    b. If the subordinating conjunction **daß** is understood, the dependent clause has *normal* word order.

Er sagt, daß er krank gewesen ist.	He says that he has been sick.
Er sagt, er ist krank gewesen.	He says he has been sick.

    c. If **wenn** is omitted from a conditional clause, the clause has *inverted* word order.

Wenn ich genug Geld hätte, ginge ich ins Kino.	If I had enough money, I would go to the movies.
Hätte ich genug Geld, so (dann) ginge ich ins Kino.	

    d. If **ob** or **wenn** is omitted from the combination **als ob** or **als wenn,** the clause has *inverted* word order.

Er sah aus, als ob (als wenn) er geschlafen hätte.	He looked as if he had slept.
Er sah aus, als hätte er geschlafen.	

    e. When a complex sentence begins with a dependent clause, the independent clause has *inverted* word order.

Wenn Sie fleißiger studiert hätten, wären Sie nicht durchgefallen.	If you had studied more diligently, you would not have failed.

f. When a dependent clause has the double infinitive construction, the conjugated verb form has to stand immediately in front of the double infinitive.

Er behauptete, daß er nie in die Stadt hätte gehen sollen.	He claimed that he never should have gone to town.

2. Relative clauses

The conjugated verb form stands at the end of a relative clause introduced by **welcher, der,** the prepositional compounds **wovon, womit, worin,** etc. (used when the relative pronoun object of a preposition refers to a thing), or the indefinite relative pronouns **wer** and **was.**

Der Mann, der (welcher) hier ist, geht morgen nach Hause.	The man who is here is going home tomorrow.
Das Buch, worin ich gelesen habe, ist sehr interessant.	The book in which I have been reading is very interesting.
Wer jeden Tag fleißig arbeitet, wird gute Noten bekommen.	Whoever works diligently every day will get good grades.
Was er in der Hand hatte, konnte ich nicht sehen.	What he had in his hand I couldn't see.

3. Indirect questions

Indirect questions introduced by subordinating elements such as **ob, was für ein, wieviele, wer, warum, was, woher, wovon,** etc. have the conjugated verb form at the end of the clause.

Ich weiß nicht, ob er heute in die Stadt geht.	I do not know if (whether) he is going to town today.
Ich weiß nicht, wer den Brief geschrieben hat.	I do not know who wrote the letter.
Der Lehrer fragt, was für ein Buch ich in der Hand habe.	The teacher asks what kind of book I have in my hand.
Die Studenten fragen, warum sie immer so viel studieren müssen.	The students ask why they always have to study so much.
Ich sah nicht, was er in der Hand hatte.	I did not see what he had in his hand.

Summary

1. Normal word order pattern.

Subject	Verb	Object	Adverbs	Complements
		Indirect object precedes direct unless direct is a personal pronoun.	Time precedes all other adverbs. General precedes specific. Time may precede noun objects.	predicate noun predicate adj. adverb separable prefix infinitive perfect participle

2. Inverted word order differs from the pattern only in the position of the conjugated verb form, which must precede the subject.

3. Transposed word order differs from the pattern only in the position of the conjugated verb form, which must stand at the end of the clause.

CATEGORIES OF STRONG VERBS

A subject of historical interest is the traditional grouping of strong verbs into seven classes based on vowel gradation, or *Ablautsreihen*. Although there is no way to avoid learning verbs individually, the following table is presented to show the seven patterns of *Ablaut*. Because of historical changes, a number of verbs that formerly fit one of the seven patterns must now be listed as exceptions to the patterns.

I, a.	**schreiben**	**schrieb**	**geschrieben**
	steigen	**stieg**	**gestiegen**
I, b.	**gleiten**	**glitt**	**geglitten**
	pfeifen	**pfiff**	**gepfiffen**
II.	**bieten**	**bot**	**geboten**
	lügen	**log**	**gelogen**
	heben	**hob**	**gehoben**
III, a.	**finden**	**fand**	**gefunden**
	singen	**sang**	**gesungen**
III, b.	**beginnen**	**begann**	**begonnen**
	schwimmen	**schwamm**	**geschwommen**

IV.	befehlen (befiehlt)	befahl	befohlen
	helfen (hilft)	half	geholfen
	nehmen (nimmt)	nahm	genommen
V.	bitten	bat	gebeten
	liegen	lag	gelegen
	lesen (liest)	las	gelesen
	geben (gibt)	gab	gegeben
VI.	fahren (fährt)	fuhr	gefahren
	graben (gräbt)	grub	gegraben
VII.	fangen (fängt)	fing	gefangen
	laufen (läuft)	lief	gelaufen
	heißen	hieß	geheißen
	stoßen (stößt)	stieß	gestoßen
	rufen	rief	gerufen
VIII.	Unclassifiable		
	gehen	ging	gegangen
	schwören	schwur	geschworen
	sein	war	gewesen
	stehen	stand	gestanden
	tun	tat	getan
	werden (wird)	wurde	geworden

PRINCIPAL PARTS OF COMMON STRONG AND IRREGULAR VERBS

Compounds with separable prefixes are not listed; for **anfangen** see **fangen,** etc. Compounds with inseparable prefixes are listed only for those verbs which do not exist in the absence of the prefix; for **bekennen** see **kennen,** but **gelingen, geschehen** and **vergessen** are given. **Befehlen** and **empfehlen** are both listed because they do not resemble the weak **fehlen.**

When the past subjunctive has alternate forms, the more common or preferred form is given first.

INFIN.	PRES. IND.	PAST IND.	PRES. PERF. IND.	PAST SUBJ.	MEANING
backen	bäckt	buk	hat gebacken	büke	bake
befehlen	befiehlt	befahl	hat befohlen	beföhle (befähle)	command
beginnen	beginnt	begann	hat begonnen	begönne (begänne)	begin
beißen	beißt	biß	hat gebissen	bisse	bite
bergen	birgt	barg	hat geborgen	bürge (bärge)	secure
biegen	biegt	bog	hat gebogen	böge	bend
biegen	biegt	bog	ist gebogen	böge	turn
bieten	bietet	bot	hat geboten	böte	offer
binden	bindet	band	hat gebunden	bände	tie
bitten	bittet	bat	hat gebeten	bäte	ask for
blasen	bläst	blies	hat geblasen	bliese	blow

135

INFIN.	PRES. IND.	PAST IND.	PRES. PERF. IND.	PAST SUBJ.	MEANING
bleiben	bleibt	blieb	ist geblieben	bliebe	remain
braten	brät	briet	hat gebraten	briete	roast
brechen	bricht	brach	hat gebrochen	bräche	break
brennen	brennt	brannte	hat gebrannt	brennte	burn
bringen	bringt	brachte	hat gebracht	brächte	bring
denken	denkt	dachte	hat gedacht	dächte	think
dringen	dringt	drang	hat gedrungen	dränge	insist
dringen	dringt	drang	ist gedrungen	dränge	penetrate
dürfen	darf	durfte	hat gedurft	dürfte	be allowed
empfehlen	empfiehlt	empfahl	hat empfohlen	empföhle (empfähle)	recommend
essen	ißt	aß	hat gegessen	äße	eat
fahren	fährt	fuhr	ist gefahren	führe	travel
fallen	fällt	fiel	ist gefallen	fiele	fall
fangen	fängt	fing	hat gefangen	finge	catch
finden	findet	fand	hat gefunden	fände	find
fliegen	fliegt	flog	ist geflogen	flöge	fly
fliehen	flieht	floh	ist geflohen	flöhe	flee
fließen	fließt	floß	ist geflossen	flösse	flow
fressen	frißt	fraß	hat gefressen	fräße	eat
frieren	friert	fror	hat gefroren	fröre	chill
frieren	friert	fror	ist gefroren	fröre	become frozen
gebären	gebiert	gebar	hat geboren	gebäre	bear
geben	gibt	gab	hat gegeben	gäbe	give
gehen	geht	ging	ist gegangen	ginge	walk
gelingen	gelingt	gelang	ist gelungen	gelänge	succeed
gelten	gilt	galt	hat gegolten	gölte (gälte)	be valid
genießen	genießt	genoß	hat genossen	genösse	enjoy
geschehen	geschieht	geschah	ist geschehen	geschähe	happen
gewinnen	gewinnt	gewann	hat gewonnen	gewönne (gewänne)	win
gießen	gießt	goß	hat gegossen	gösse	pour
gleichen	gleicht	glich	hat geglichen	gliche	equal
gleiten	gleitet	glitt	ist geglitten	glitte	slide
graben	gräbt	grub	hat gegraben	grübe	dig
greifen	greift	griff	hat gegriffen	griffe	grasp
haben	hat	hatte	hat gehabt	hätte	have
halten	hält	hielt	hat gehalten	hielte	hold

INFIN.	PRES. IND.	PAST IND.	PRES. PERF. IND.	PAST SUBJ.	MEANING
hängen*	hängt	hing	hat gehangen	hinge	hang
hauen	haut	hieb	hat gehauen	hiebe	cut
heben	hebt	hob	hat gehoben	höbe	lift
heißen	heißt	hieß	hat geheißen	hieße	be named
helfen	hilft	half	hat geholfen	hülfe (hälfe)	help
kennen	kennt	kannte	hat gekannt	kennte	know
klingen	klingt	klang	hat geklungen	klänge	sound
kommen	kommt	kam	ist gekommen	käme	come
können	kann	konnte	hat gekonnt	könnte	be able
kriechen	kriecht	kroch	ist gekrochen	kröche	creep
laden	lädt	lud	hat geladen	lüde	load
lassen	läßt	ließ	hat gelassen	ließe	let
laufen	läuft	lief	ist gelaufen	liefe	run
leiden	leidet	litt	hat gelitten	litte	suffer
leihen	leiht	lieh	hat geliehen	liehe	lend
lesen	liest	las	hat gelesen	läse	read
liegen	liegt	lag	hat gelegen	läge	lie
löschen	lischt	losch	ist geloschen	lösche	be extinguished
lügen	lügt	log	hat gelogen	löge	tell a lie
meiden	meidet	mied	hat gemieden	miede	avoid
messen	mißt	maß	hat gemessen	mäße	measure
mögen	mag	mochte	hat gemocht	möchte	like
müssen	muß	mußte	hat gemußt	müßte	have to
nehmen	nimmt	nahm	hat genommen	nähme	take
nennen	nennt	nannte	hat genannt	nennte	name
pfeifen	pfeift	pfiff	hat gepfiffen	pfiffe	whistle
preisen	preist	pries	hat gepriesen	priese	praise
raten	rät	riet	hat geraten	riete	advise
reiben	reibt	rieb	hat gerieben	riebe	rub
reißen	reißt	riß	hat gerissen	risse	tear
reiten	reitet	ritt	ist geritten	ritte	ride
rennen	rennt	rannte	ist gerannt	rennte	run
riechen	riecht	roch	hat gerochen	röche	smell
rufen	ruft	rief	hat gerufen	riefe	call
schaffen	schafft	schuf	hat geschaffen	schüfe	create
scheiden	scheidet	schied	hat geschieden	schiede	separate
scheiden	scheidet	schied	ist geschieden	schiede	(de)part

* **Hängen** has displaced the strong intransitive infinitive **hangen**. The present tense forms of **hangen** have practically disappeared but are found in older literature and in dialects. The transitive **hängen** is weak.

INFIN.	PRES. IND.	PAST IND.	PRES. PERF. IND.	PAST SUBJ.	MEANING
scheinen	scheint	schien	hat geschienen	schiene	shine
schelten	schilt	schalt	hat gescholten	schölte (schälte)	scold
schieben	schiebt	schob	hat geschoben	schöbe	push
schießen	schießt	schoß	hat geschossen	schösse	shoot
schlafen	schläft	schlief	hat geschlafen	schliefe	sleep
schlagen	schlägt	schlug	hat geschlagen	schlüge	hit
schleichen	schleicht	schlich	ist geschlichen	schliche	creep
schließen	schließt	schloß	hat geschlossen	schlösse	close
schlingen	schlingt	schlang	hat geschlungen	schlänge	entwine
schmeißen	schmeißt	schmiß	hat geschmissen	schmisse	hurl
schmelzen	schmilzt	schmolz	ist geschmolzen	schmölze	melt
schneiden	schneidet	schnitt	hat geschnitten	schnitte	cut
schrecken	schrickt	schrak	ist geschrocken*	schräke	be(come) frightened
schreiben	schreibt	schrieb	hat geschrieben	schriebe	write
schreien	schreit	schrie	hat geschrie(e)n	schriee	scream
schreiten	schreitet	schritt	ist geschritten	schritte	step
schweigen	schweigt	schwieg	hat geschwiegen	schwiege	be silent
schwellen	schwillt	schwoll	ist geschwollen	schwölle	swell
schwimmen	schwimmt	schwamm	ist geschwommen	schwömme (schwämme)	swim
schwinden	schwindet	schwand	ist geschwunden	schwände	vanish
schwingen	schwingt	schwang	hat geschwungen	schwänge	swing
schwören	schwört	schwur	hat geschworen	schwüre	swear
sehen	sieht	sah	hat gesehen	sähe	see
sein	ist	war	ist gewesen	wäre	be
senden	sendet	sandte	hat gesandt	sendete	send
singen	singt	sang	hat gesungen	sänge	sing
sinken	sinkt	sank	ist gesunken	sänke	sink
sinnen	sinnt	sann	hat gesonnen	sänne (sönne)	think
sitzen	sitzt	saß	hat gesessen	säße	sit
sollen	soll	sollte	hat gesollt	sollte	be supposed to
speien	speit	spie	hat gespie(e)n	spiee	spit
spinnen	spinnt	spann	hat gesponnen	spönne (spänne)	spin
sprechen	spricht	sprach	hat gesprochen	spräche	speak

* Replaced by **erschrocken. Erschrecken** is more common than **schrecken** in all forms. The transitive **(er)schrecken** *to frighten* is weak.

INFIN.	PRES. IND.	PAST IND.	PRES. PERF. IND.	PAST SUBJ.	MEANING
springen	springt	sprang	ist gesprungen	spränge	leap
stechen	sticht	stach	hat gestochen	stäche	sting
stehen	steht	stand	hat gestanden	stände (stünde)	stand
stehlen	stiehlt	stahl	hat gestohlen	stöhle (stähle)	steal
steigen	steigt	stieg	ist gestiegen	stiege	climb
sterben	stirbt	starb	ist gestorben	stürbe	die
stoßen	stößt	stieß	hat gestoßen	stieße	push
streichen	streicht	strich	hat gestrichen	striche	stroke
streiten	streitet	stritt	hat gestritten	stritte	quarrel
tragen	trägt	trug	hat getragen	trüge	carry
treffen	trifft	traf	hat getroffen	träfe	hit
treiben	treibt	trieb	hat getrieben	triebe	drive
treten	tritt	trat	hat getreten	träte	kick
treten	tritt	trat	ist getreten	träte	step
trinken	trinkt	trank	hat getrunken	tränke	drink
trügen	trügt	trog	hat getrogen	tröge	deceive
tun	tut	tat	hat getan	täte	do
verdrießen	verdrießt	verdroß	hat verdrossen	verdrösse	displease
vergessen	vergißt	vergaß	hat vergessen	vergäße	forget
verlieren	verliert	verlor	hat verloren	verlöre	lose
wachsen	wächst	wuchs	ist gewachsen	wüchse	grow
wägen	wägt	wog	hat gewogen	wöge	weigh
waschen	wäscht	wusch	hat gewaschen	wüsche	wash
weichen	weicht	wich	ist gewichen	wiche	yield
weisen	weist	wies	hat gewiesen	wiese	show
wenden	wendet	wandte	hat gewandt	wendete	turn
werben	wirbt	warb	hat geworben	würbe	woo
werden	wird	wurde	ist geworden	würde	become
werfen	wirft	warf	hat geworfen	würfe	throw
wiegen	wiegt	wog	hat gewogen	wöge	weigh
winden	windet	wand	hat gewunden	wände	wind
wissen	weiß	wußte	hat gewußt	wüßte	know
wollen	will	wollte	hat gewollt	wollte	want (to)
zeihen	zeiht	zieh	hat geziehen	ziehe	accuse
ziehen	zieht	zog	hat gezogen	zöge	pull
ziehen	zieht	zog	ist gezogen	zöge	move
zwingen	zwingt	zwang	hat gezwungen	zwänge	force

VERB PARADIGMS

A. Strong Verb

PRINCIPAL PARTS: **nehmen**   **nimmt**   **nahm**   **hat genommen**

INFINITIVES: ACTIVE   PASSIVE

   PRESENT   **nehmen**   **genommen werden**
   PERFECT (*or* PAST)   **genommen haben**   **genommen worden sein**

1. Active Voice

	PRESENT		SIMPLE PAST
INDICATIVE	SUBJUNCTIVE	INDICATIVE	SUBJUNCTIVE
ich nehme	ich nehme	ich nahm	ich nähme
du nimmst	du nehmest	du nahmst	du nähmest
er nimmt	er nehme	er nahm	er nähme
wir nehmen	wir nehmen	wir nahmen	wir nähmen
ihr nehmt	ihr nehmet	ihr nahmt	ihr nähmet
sie nehmen	sie nehmen	sie nahmen	sie nähmen

PRESENT PERFECT

INDICATIVE	SUBJUNCTIVE
ich habe genommen	ich habe genommen
du hast genommen	du habest genommen
er hat genommen, etc.	er habe genommen, etc.

PAST PERFECT

INDICATIVE

ich hatte genommen

du hattest genommen

er hatte genommen, etc.

SUBJUNCTIVE

ich hätte genommen

du hättest genommen

er hätte genommen, etc.

FUTURE

INDICATIVE

ich werde nehmen

du wirst nehmen

er wird nehmen, etc.

SUBJUNCTIVE

ich werde nehmen

du werdest nehmen

er werde nehmen, etc.

FUTURE PERFECT

INDICATIVE

ich werde genommen haben

du wirst genommen haben

er wird genommen haben, etc.

SUBJUNCTIVE

ich werde genommen haben

du werdest genommen haben

er werde genommen haben, etc.

PRESENT CONDITIONAL

ich würde nehmen

du würdest nehmen

er würde nehmen, etc.

PAST CONDITIONAL

ich würde genommen haben

du würdest genommen haben

er würde genommen haben, etc.

2. Passive Voice

PRESENT

INDICATIVE

ich werde genommen

du wirst genommen

er wird genommen, etc.

SUBJUNCTIVE

ich werde genommen

du werdest genommen

er werde genommen, etc.

SIMPLE PAST

INDICATIVE

ich wurde genommen
du wurdest genommen
er wurde genommen, etc.

SUBJUNCTIVE

ich würde genommen
du würdest genommen
er würde genommen, etc.

PRESENT PERFECT

INDICATIVE

ich bin genommen worden
du bist genommen worden
er ist genommen worden, etc.

SUBJUNCTIVE

ich sei genommen worden
du seiest genommen worden
er sei genommen worden, etc.

PAST PERFECT

INDICATIVE

ich war genommen worden
du warst genommen worden
er war genommen worden, etc.

SUBJUNCTIVE

ich wäre genommen worden
du wärest genommen worden
er wäre genommen worden, etc.

FUTURE

INDICATIVE

ich werde genommen werden
du wirst genommen werden
er wird genommen werden, etc.

SUBJUNCTIVE

ich werde genommen werden
du werdest genommen werden
er werde genommen werden, etc.

FUTURE PERFECT

INDICATIVE

ich werde genommen worden sein
du wirst genommen worden sein
er wird genommen worden sein,
   etc.

SUBJUNCTIVE

ich werde genommen worden sein
du werdest genommen worden sein
er werde genommen worden sein,
   etc.

PRESENT CONDITIONAL	PAST CONDITIONAL
ich würde genommen werden	ich würde genommen worden sein
du würdest genommen werden	du würdest genommen worden sein
er würde genommen werden, etc.	er würde genommen worden sein, etc.

B. Weak Verb

PRINCIPAL PARTS:	fragen	fragt	fragte	hat gefragt

INFINITIVES:	ACTIVE	PASSIVE
PRESENT	fragen	gefragt werden
PERFECT (*or* PAST)	gefragt haben	gefragt worden sein

1. Active Voice

PRESENT / SIMPLE PAST

INDICATIVE	SUBJUNCTIVE	INDICATIVE	SUBJUNCTIVE
ich frage	ich frage	ich fragte	ich fragte
du fragst	du fragest	du fragtest	du fragtest
er fragt	er frage	er fragte	er fragte
wir fragen	wir fragen	wir fragten	wir fragten
ihr fragt	ihr fraget	ihr fragtet	ihr fragtet
sie fragen	sie fragen	sie fragten	sie fragten

PRESENT PERFECT

INDICATIVE	SUBJUNCTIVE
ich habe gefragt	ich habe gefragt
du hast gefragt	du habest gefragt
er hat gefragt, etc.	er habe gefragt, etc.

PAST PERFECT

INDICATIVE

ich hatte gefragt
du hattest gefragt
er hatte gefragt, etc.

SUBJUNCTIVE

ich hätte gefragt
du hättest gefragt
er hätte gefragt, etc.

FUTURE

INDICATIVE

ich werde fragen
du wirst fragen
er wird fragen, etc.

SUBJUNCTIVE

ich werde fragen
du werdest fragen
er werde fragen, etc.

FUTURE PERFECT

INDICATIVE

ich werde gefragt haben
du wirst gefragt haben
er wird gefragt haben, etc.

SUBJUNCTIVE

ich werde gefragt haben
du werdest gefragt haben
er werde gefragt haben, etc.

PRESENT CONDITIONAL

ich würde fragen
du würdest fragen
er würde fragen, etc.

PAST CONDITIONAL

ich würde gefragt haben
du würdest gefragt haben
er würde gefragt haben, etc.

2. Passive Voice

PRESENT

INDICATIVE

ich werde gefragt
du wirst gefragt
er wird gefragt, etc.

SUBJUNCTIVE

ich werde gefragt
du werdest gefragt
er werde gefragt, etc.

SIMPLE PAST

INDICATIVE

ich wurde gefragt
du wurdest gefragt
er wurde gefragt, etc.

SUBJUNCTIVE

ich würde gefragt
du würdest gefragt
er würde gefragt, etc.

PRESENT PERFECT

INDICATIVE

ich bin gefragt worden
du bist gefragt worden
er ist gefragt worden, etc.

SUBJUNCTIVE

ich sei gefragt worden
du seiest gefragt worden
er sei gefragt worden, etc.

PAST PERFECT

INDICATIVE

ich war gefragt worden
du warst gefragt worden
er war gefragt worden, etc.

SUBJUNCTIVE

ich wäre gefragt worden
du wärest gefragt worden
er wäre gefragt worden, etc.

FUTURE

INDICATIVE

ich werde gefragt werden
du wirst gefragt werden
er wird gefragt werden, etc.

SUBJUNCTIVE

ich werde gefragt werden
du werdest gefragt werden
er werde gefragt werden, etc.

FUTURE PERFECT

INDICATIVE

ich werde gefragt worden sein
du wirst gefragt worden sein
er wird gefragt worden sein, etc.

SUBJUNCTIVE

ich werde gefragt worden sein
du werdest gefragt worden sein
er werde gefragt worden sein, etc.

PRESENT CONDITIONAL

ich würde gefragt werden
du würdest gefragt werden
er würde gefragt werden, etc.

PAST CONDITIONAL

ich würde gefragt worden sein
du würdest gefragt worden sein
er würde gefragt worden sein, etc.

C. Modal Auxiliary

PRINCIPAL PARTS: **können   kann   konnte   hat gekonnt**

INFINITIVES:	PRESENT	PERFECT (*or* PAST)
	können	**gekonnt haben**

	PRESENT		SIMPLE PAST
INDICATIVE	SUBJUNCTIVE	INDICATIVE	SUBJUNCTIVE
ich kann	ich könne	ich konnte	ich könnte
du kannst	du könnest	du konntest	du könntest
er kann	er könne	er konnte	er könnte
wir können	wir können	wir konnten	wir könnten
ihr könnt	ihr könnet	ihr konntet	ihr könntet
sie können	sie können	sie konnten	sie könnten

PRESENT PERFECT WITHOUT COMPLEMENTARY INFINITIVE

INDICATIVE	SUBJUNCTIVE
ich habe gekonnt	ich habe gekonnt
du hast gekonnt	du habest gekonnt
er hat gekonnt, etc.	er habe gekonnt, etc.

PRESENT PERFECT WITH COMPLEMENTARY INFINITIVE

INDICATIVE	SUBJUNCTIVE
ich habe gehen können	ich habe gehen können
du hast gehen können	du habest gehen können
er hat gehen können, etc.	er habe gehen können, etc.

PAST PERFECT WITHOUT COMPLEMENTARY INFINITIVE

INDICATIVE

ich hatte gekonnt
du hattest gekonnt
er hatte gekonnt, etc.

SUBJUNCTIVE

ich hätte gekonnt
du hättest gekonnt
er hätte gekonnt, etc.

PAST PERFECT WITH COMPLEMENTARY INFINITIVE

INDICATIVE

ich hatte gehen können
du hattest gehen können
er hatte gehen können, etc.

SUBJUNCTIVE

ich hätte gehen können
du hättest gehen können
er hätte gehen können, etc.

FUTURE

INDICATIVE

ich werde können
du wirst können
er wird können, etc.

SUBJUNCTIVE

ich werde können
du werdest können
er werde können, etc.

FUTURE PERFECT WITHOUT COMPLEMENTARY INFINITIVE

INDICATIVE

ich werde gekonnt haben
du wirst gekonnt haben
er wird gekonnt haben, etc.

SUBJUNCTIVE

ich werde gekonnt haben
du werdest gekonnt haben
er werde gekonnt haben, etc.

FUTURE PERFECT WITH COMPLEMENTARY INFINITIVE

INDICATIVE

ich werde haben gehen können
du wirst haben gehen können
er wird haben gehen können, etc.

SUBJUNCTIVE

ich werde haben gehen können
du werdest haben gehen können
er werde haben gehen können, etc.

ENGLISH–GERMAN VOCABULARY

All words needed for the English-to-German exercises are listed, the only exceptions being numerals, personal pronouns, and reflexive pronouns. Masculine and neuter nouns are given with their genitive singular and nominative plural, feminine nouns with their plural only. Strong and irregular verbs are indicated by an asterisk, and the auxiliary **ist** is added when applicable. Verbs with the variable prefixes **über-** and **unter-** are separable unless otherwise indicated.

able: be — to können*

about über + *acc.*, von; = **approximately** ungefähr

absent abwesend

accident der Unfall, –s, ⸗e

according to nach

accustomed: become — to sich gewöhnen an + *acc.*

acid die Säure, –n

acquainted: become — (with each other) sich kennenlernen

across über

act handeln, tun*

address die Adresse, –n

admire bewundern

advice der Rat, –es

advise raten*

afraid: be — of sich fürchten vor + *dat.*

Africa (das) Afrika, –s

after *prep.* nach; *conj.* nachdem

afternoon der Nachmittag, –s, –e; **in the —** am Nachmittag, nachmittags

again wieder, noch einmal; **— and —** immer wieder

against gegen

ago vor + *dat.*

agreeable angenehm

air die Luft

airplane das Flugzeug, –s, –e

alive lebend

all ganz; *pl.* alle; = **everything** alles; **— day (evening)** den ganzen Tag (Abend)

allowed: be — to dürfen*

149

almost fast

Alps die Alpen (*pl.*)

already schon

also auch

although obgleich, obwohl

always immer

America (das) Amerika, –s

American *adj.* amerikanisch

and und

angry ärgerlich

animal das Tier, –es, –e

annoyed: be — at sich ärgern über +
acc.

another noch ein

answer antworten; the — (to) die
Antwort (auf + *acc.*)

anyone else irgend ein anderer

anything: not — nichts

anyway jedenfalls, immerhin

apple der Apfel, –s, ⸚; — tree der
Apfelbaum, –s, ⸚e

apply for sich bewerben* um

approach sich nähern + *dat.*

April der April, –s

arm der Arm, –es, –e

around um

arrive ankommen* (ist)

article der Artikel, –s, –

as als; = when als; — if als ob, als
wenn; — old — so alt wie

ask fragen; — a question eine Frage
stellen; — for bitten* um

assignment die Hausaufgabe, –n

astronomy die Astronomie

at an, bei; at (*time by clock*) um

attend beiwohnen + *dat.*; — a lecture
eine Vorlesung hören

attentive aufmerksam

aunt die Tante, –n

axis die Achse, –n

baby kleines Kind, –es, –er

back der Rücken, –s, –

baggage das Gepäck, –s

bake backen*

baker der Bäcker, –s, –

barefoot barfuß

be sein* (ist); To be or not to be Sein
oder Nichtsein

bear der Bär, –en, –en

beard der Bart, –es, ⸚e

beat schlagen*

beautiful schön

beaver der Biber, –s, –

because weil; — of wegen + *gen.*

become werden*, werden zu, (ist)

bed das Bett, –es, –en

before *prep.* vor; *conj.* ehe, bevor

begin anfangen*, beginnen*

beginning der Anfang, –s, ⸚e

behind hinter

believe glauben

belong (to) gehören + *dat.*

bend down sich bücken

beside neben

best: the — das Beste; *adv.* am besten

better besser

between zwischen

big groß

bird der Vogel, –s, ⸚

birthday: for (my, his, etc.) — zum
Geburtstag

bit: a — ein wenig, ein bißchen

black schwarz

blackboard die Wandtafel, –n

blow blasen*

board (blackboard) die Wandtafel, −n
boast (of) sich rühmen + *gen.*
book das Buch, −es, ⁼er
born geboren
borrow (from) (einem) abborgen
both beide
bottle die Flasche, −n
bow sich verbeugen
boy der Junge, −n, −n
brave tapfer
bread das Brot, −es, −e
breakfast das Frühstück, −s, −e
bright hell
bring bringen*; — **along** mitbringen*,
mitnehmen*
broken (to pieces) zerbrochen
brook der Bach, −es, ⁼e
brother der Bruder, −s, ⁼
brown braun
build bauen
building das Gebäude, −s, −
bullet die Kugel, −n
but aber
buy kaufen
by (*persons*) von; — (*car, train, etc.*) mit;
— (+ *doing something*) indem (+ *sub-*
ject and verb)

call rufen*
can können*; **it — be found** es läßt
sich finden
car der Wagen, −s, −; das Auto, −s, −s
cards: play — Karten spielen
careful vorsichtig
carry tragen*
castle das Schloß, −es, ⁼er
cat die Katze, −n
catch fangen*; — **a cold** sich erkälten

century das Jahrhundert, −s, −e
certificate der Schein, −es, −e
chair der Stuhl, −es, ⁼e
change (sich) ändern, (sich) verändern
cheap billig
check (bill) die Rechnung, −en
cheerful heiter, fröhlich
cherry tree der Kirschbaum, −s, ⁼e
child das Kind, −es, −er
choice die Wahl, −en
church die Kirche, −n
cigarette die Zigarette, −n
cinema das Kino, −s, −s
city die Stadt, ⁼e
claim (assert) behaupten
class die Klasse, −n
classroom das Klassenzimmer, −s, −
clench ballen
client der Klient, −en, −en
climate das Klima, −s
climb in einsteigen* (ist)
cloth das Tuch, −es, ⁼er
clothes die Kleider (*pl.*)
coat der Mantel, −s, ⁼; der Rock, −es, ⁼e
cold kalt; **catch a —** sich erkälten
come kommen* (ist); — **back** zurückkommen* (ist); — **out** herauskom-
men* (ist), hinauskommen* (ist)
comfortable bequem
command befehlen*
company die Gesellschaft, −en
complete vollenden
complex kompliziert
condition der Zustand, −s, ⁼e
congratulate (on) gratulieren (zu) +
dat.
consider überlegen (*insep.*)
constantly immer

contain enthalten*
continue (with) fortfahren* (mit)
contrary to gegen
converse sich unterhalten* (*insep.*)
cool kühl
corner die Ecke, –n
correct richtig
country(side) das Land, –es, ̈er; **to the —** aufs Land
course der Kurs, –es, –e
cousin der Vetter, –s, –n; die Kusine, –n
crooked krumm
cross überqueren (*insep.*)
crowd die Menge, –n
cry schreien*
cup die Tasse, –n
custom der Brauch, –es, ̈e; die Sitte, –n
cut schneiden*

danger die Gefahr, –en
dark dunkel
dative der Dativ, –s
daughter die Tochter, ̈
day der Tag, –es, –e
dead tot
decide sich entscheiden*
deed die Tat, –en
deep tief
definite bestimmt
depend on sich verlassen* auf + *acc.*
describe beschreiben*
desk der Schreibtisch, –es, –e
destination der Bestimmungsort, –s, –e
detail die Einzelheit, –en
dictionary das Wörterbuch, –s, ̈er
die sterben* (ist)
different verschieden, ander–
difficult schwer

difficulty die Schwierigkeit, –en
diligent fleißig
dining room das Eßzimmer, –s, –
dinner das Abendessen, –s
disappear verschwinden* (ist)
discover entdecken
discuss besprechen*
do tun*, machen
doctor der Arzt, –es, ̈e; der Doktor, –s, –en
dog der Hund, –es, –e
downtown *adv.* in die Stadt
dress das Kleid, –es, –er
drink trinken*
drive fahren* (ist); **— around** herumfahren* (ist); **— up** herfahren* (ist)
driver der Fahrer, –s, –
during während

each jeder, jede, jedes; **— other** einander, sich
ear das Ohr, –es, –en
early früh
earth die Erde, –n
Eastern Zone die Ostzone
easy leicht
eat essen*
education die Ausbildung
egg das Ei, –es, –er
eighth das Achtel, –s, –
elderly älter–
elephant der Elefant, –en, –en
employee der Angestellte, –n, –n
end das Ende, –s, –n
enemy der Feind, –es, –e; die Feindin, –nen
English (das) Englisch; **in —** im Englischen, auf englisch

enjoy genießen*

enough genug

entire ganz

error der Irrtum, –s, ‷er; der Fehler,
  –s, –

escape ent– + *various verbs:* entlaufen*
  (ist), entkommen* (ist), entgehen*
  (ist), entfliehen* (ist)

even selbst

evening der Abend, –s, –e; **in the —**
  abends, am Abend

ever je

every jeder, jede, jedes

everybody jeder, jedermann

everything alles

everywhere überall

exactly genau

examine untersuchen (*insep*).

example das Beispiel, –s, –e; das
  Vorbild, –s, –er

exceedingly äußerst

excuse entschuldigen

excuse die Entschuldigung, –en

exercise die Übung, –en

expect erwarten

expectation die Erwartung, –en

expensive teuer

experiment der Versuch, –s, –e

explain erklären

explanation die Erklärung, –en

eye das Auge, –s, –n

face: come — to — with gegen-
  übertreten* (ist) + *dat.*

fact die Tatsache, –n; **the — that** daß *or*
  da-*compound*, daß

factory die Fabrik, –en

fairy tale das Märchen, –s, –

fall (autumn) der Herbst, –es, –e

fall fallen* (ist)

familiar bekannt

family die Familie, –n

famous berühmt

far weit; **the farther, the better** je
  weiter, desto besser

farmer der Bauer, –s *or* –n, –n

fast schnell

father der Vater, –s, ‷

feel (well) sich (wohl) befinden*, sich
  (wohl) fühlen

few, a few einige, ein paar

field das Feld, –es, –er

figure die Gestalt, –en

find finden*; **— out** erfahren*

finish beenden, fertig machen

first der erste; **in the — place** erstens

fist die Faust, ‷e

fit passen + *dat.*

flower die Blume, –n

fly fliegen* (ist)

foolishness die Torheit

foot der Fuß, –es, ‷e; **on —** zu Fuß

footpath der Fußpfad, –s, –e

for für; **— a year** seit einem Jahr

foreign language die Fremdsprache, –n

forest der Wald, –es, ‷er

forget vergessen*

form die Form, –en

former früher; **the —** jener, jene, jenes

fortunately zum Glück, glücklicherweise

fourth *adj.* der vierte; *noun* das Viertel,
  –s, –

fresh frisch

friend der Freund, –es, –e

from von, aus; **— here** von hier aus

furnace der Gasofen, –s, ‷

garden der Garten, –s, ⸚; **— wall** die Gartenmauer, –n

general der General, –s, –e *or* ⸚e

gentleman der Herr, –n, –en

German *adj.* deutsch

German (language) (das) Deutsch; **in —** auf deutsch, im Deutschen; **into —** ins Deutsche

Germany (das) Deutschland

get = acquire bekommen*; **= become** werden* (ist); **— out** aussteigen* (ist); **— up** aufstehen* (ist)

giraffe die Giraffe, –n

girl das Mädchen, –s, –; das Fräulein, –s, –

give geben*

glass das Glas, –es, ⸚er

go gehen* (ist); **— for a walk** einen Spaziergang machen, spazierengehen* (ist); **— and get again** wiederholen

goal das Ziel, –es, –e

good gut

grammatical grammatisch

grandfather der Großvater, –s, ⸚

great groß

green grün

ground der Boden, –s, ⸚

grow wachsen* (ist)

guide der Führer, –s, –; der Leiter, –s, –

half *adj.* halb; *noun* die Hälfte, –n

hand die Hand, ⸚e

handsome schön

hang hängen*

happen geschehen* (ist)

harbor der Hafen, –s, ⸚

hard schwer; **study —** fleißig studieren; **— wind** starker Wind

harvest die Ernte, –n

hat der Hut, –es, ⸚e

have haben*; **— to** müssen*; **— a good time** sich amüsieren; **— built** bauen lassen*

head der Kopf, –es, ⸚e

hear hören

heat heizen

help helfen* + *dat.;* die Hilfe

her ihr

here hier

hidden: be — verborgen liegen*

high hoch

his sein

hit schlagen*; **be — by a car** überfahren werden*

hit der Schlager, –s, –

hold halten*; **— a meeting** eine Versammlung abhalten*

home *adv.* nach Hause; **at —** zu Hause

homework die Hausaufgabe, –n

honor ehren

hope hoffen

hot heiß

hour die Stunde, –n

house das Haus, –es, ⸚er

how wie; **— many** wieviele

hurry eilen (ist), sich beeilen

hurt (injure) verletzen; *intr.* weh tun* + *dat.*

if wenn; **= whether** ob

imagine sich (*dat.*) vorstellen; **it can be –d** es läßt sich denken

immediately sogleich

important wichtig

impress beeindrucken

in in + *dat.*, auf + *dat.;* — **this weather** bei diesem Wetter

individually einzeln

injured verletzt

injurious schädlich

ink die Tinte

inn das Wirtshaus, −es, ⸚er

inquire (about) sich erkundigen (nach)

insect das Insekt, −s, −en

instead of (an)statt + *gen.*

instructor der Lehrer, −s, −

intelligent intelligent

interested: be(come) — in sich interessieren für

interesting interessant

into in + *acc.;* auf + *acc.*

introduce vorstellen

invite einladen*

irregular unregelmäßig

January der Januar, −s

job die Stellung, −en

joy die Freude

judge der Richter, −s, −

July der Juli, −s

June der Juni, −s

just (now) eben

kill töten

kind die Art, −en; **all −s of** allerlei

king der König, −s, −e

kingdom das Reich, −es, −e

kitchen die Küche, −n

knife das Messer, −s, −

knight der Ritter, −s, −

know (*as fact*) wissen*; = **be acquainted with** kennen*

lady die Dame, −n

lake der See, −s, −n

language die Sprache, −n

large groß

last letzt−; — **night** diese Nacht

late spät

lately kürzlich, neulich

latter: the — dieser, diese, dieses

lawyer der Rechtsanwalt, −s, ⸚e

leading führend; — **role** die Hauptrolle, −n

leaf das Blatt, −es, ⸚er

lean out sich hinauslehnen

learn lernen

leash die Leine, −n

least am wenigsten; **at —** wenigstens

leave verlassen*; = **depart** abfahren* (ist), weggehen* (ist)

lecture die Vorlesung, −en

left: on the —, to the — links

leg das Bein, −es, −e

legend die Sage, −n

less weniger

lesson die Aufgabe, −n

let lassen*

letter der Brief, −es, −e

library die Bibliothek, −en

lie = **recline** liegen*; = **tell a —** lügen*

life das Leben, −s

light das Licht, −es, −er

like mögen*, gern haben*; — **to** mögen*, gern + *verb;* — **best** am liebsten haben*; **I — it** es gefällt* mir

lion der Löwe, −n, −n

listen zuhören

literature die Literatur

little klein

live wohnen

long *adj.* lang; *adv.* lange; — **ago** schon lange; **for a — time** lange

look: — **around** sich umsehen*; — **at** sich (*dat.*) ansehen*; — **down** hinabblicken; — **for** suchen; — **forward to** sich freuen auf + *acc.;* — **up** (— **for**) suchen

lose verlieren*; — **one's way** sich verirren

love die Liebe

lover der Liebhaber, –s, –

luck: good — das Glück, –es

lunch das Mittagessen

magazine die Zeitschrift, –en

maid das Dienstmädchen, –s, –

mail aufgeben*

make machen

man der Mann, –es, ⸚er; der Herr, –n, –en

many viele; — **a** mancher, manche, manches

map die Landkarte, –n

masculine männlich

master der Herr, –n, –en

matter die Sache, –n; **what is the —** was ist los

may dürfen*

meadow die Wiese, –n

means das Mittel, –s, –

meet treffen*, begegnen (ist) + *dat.*

meeting die Versammlung, –en

merchandise die Waren (*pl.*)

merchant der Kaufmann, –s, *pl.* die Kaufleute

midnight die Mitternacht

might = **could** könnte; = **would be permitted** dürfte

milk die Milch

minute die Minute, –n

misspell falsch buchstabieren

mistake der Fehler, –s, –

mix mischen

money das Geld, –es

monkey der Affe, –n, –n

month der Monat, –s, –e

moon der Mond, –es, –e

more mehr; — **bitter than sour** eher bitter als sauer, mehr bitter als sauer

morning der Morgen, –s, –; **in the —** am Morgen, morgens; **one —** eines Morgens; **this —** heute morgen

most der meiste

mother die Mutter, ⸚

mountain der Berg, –es, –e

movie der Film, –es, –e

movies das Kino, –s, –s

much viel, vieles

Munich (das) München

museum das Museum, –s, die Museen

music die Musik

must müssen*

my mein

name der Name, –ns, –n; nennen*

narrow schmal

near neben, bei

need bedürfen* + *gen.*

neighbor der Nachbar, –s *or* –n, –n

nest das Nest, –es, –er

never nie, niemals; — **before** noch nie

new neu

newspaper die Zeitung, –en

next nächst–; **in the — few days** in den nächsten Tagen

next to neben

nice schön; — **things** Schönes
night die Nacht, ‑e; **last** — diese Nacht
no *adj.* kein; — **longer** nicht mehr
noble edel
nobody niemand, keiner
noon der Mittag, ‑s, ‑e
not nicht; — **at all** gar nicht; — **any more** nicht mehr; — **yet** noch nicht
nothing nichts
noun das Hauptwort, ‑s, ‑er
novel der Roman, ‑s, ‑e
novelist der Romanschriftsteller, ‑s, ‑
now jetzt, nun

obey gehorchen + *dat.*
occur to einfallen* (ist) + *dat.*
o'clock Uhr
of von
offer bieten*
official der Beamte, ‑n, ‑n; ein Beamter
often oft
old alt
on (*horizontal*) auf; (*vertical*) an; — **a street** in einer Straße; (*travel*) — (*a train etc.*) mit; — **the fourth of July** am vierten Juli
once more noch einmal
one *demonstrative* einer; *indefinite* man
only nur
open öffnen, aufmachen
opera die Oper, ‑n
opinion die Meinung, ‑en
order: in — **to** um ... zu + *infinitive*
orthography die Orthographie
ostrich der Strauß, ‑es, ‑e
other ander‑
our unser
out of aus

outside draußen
over über; **be** — aus sein* (ist)

page die Seite, ‑n
painter der Maler, ‑s, ‑
painting das Gemälde, ‑s, ‑
paper das Papier, ‑s, ‑e
parents die Eltern
park der Park, ‑es, ‑e
party die Gesellschaft, ‑en
passport der Paß, ‑es, ‑e
past vergangen
patience die Geduld
pay bezahlen; — **attention** aufpassen
pear tree der Birnbaum, ‑s, ‑e
pedestrian der Fußgänger, ‑s, ‑
pen die Füllfeder, ‑n
pencil der Bleistift, ‑s, ‑e
people die Leute
perform (**deeds**) (Taten) verrichten
permit lassen*, erlauben + *dat.*
person die Person, ‑en; der Mensch, ‑en, ‑en
picture das Bild, ‑es, ‑er
pipe die Pfeife, ‑n
pistol die Pistole, ‑n
place legen, stellen
planet der Planet, ‑en, ‑en
plant die Pflanze, ‑n
plate der Teller, ‑s, ‑
play spielen
playing das Spielen, ‑s
plural form die Pluralform, ‑en
pocket die Tasche, ‑n
poem das Gedicht, ‑s, ‑e
poet der Dichter, ‑s, ‑
point at weisen* auf + *acc.*
poison das Gift, ‑es, ‑e

police die Polizei
policeman der Polizist, –en, –en
politics die Politik
poor arm
position (**job**) die Stellung, –en
possible möglich
pour gießen*
prefer lieber haben*
prepare for sich vorbereiten auf + *acc.*
present das Geschenk, –s, –e
pretty schön, hübsch
previous vorig
prince der Prinz, –en, –en
prize der Preis, –es, –e
probably wohl
professor der Professor, –s, –en
promise versprechen*
pronounce aussprechen*
proud stolz
purse die Handtasche, –n
put stecken; — **down** hinlegen

question die Frage, –n

rabbit der Hase, –n, –n
rain der Regen, –s; regnen
rather ziemlich; = **preferably** lieber
reach erreichen
read lesen*
ready bereit
reason (**cause**) der Grund, –es, ⁼e;
    die Ursache, –n
receive bekommen*, erhalten*,
    empfangen*
recognize erkennen*
recommend empfehlen*
red rot

reflexive pronoun das Reflexiv-
    pronomen, –s, Reflexivpronomina
remember sich erinnern + *gen. or* an
    + *acc.*
remind (**of**) erinnern (an + *acc.*)
report der Bericht, –s, –e; berichten
require brauchen
resemble ähneln + *dat.*
restaurant das Restaurant, –s, –s
return (**come back**) zurückkommen*
    (ist)
revolve sich drehen
Rhine der Rhein, –s
rich reich
rid: get — of loswerden* (ist)
right: — after gerade nach; — **away**
    sogleich
ring der Ring, –es, –e
rise aufgehen* (ist)
robber der Räuber, –s, –
role die Rolle, –n
roll das Brötchen, –s, –
room das Zimmer, –s, –
row die Reihe, –n
run laufen* (ist); — **across** hinüber-
    laufen* (ist), herüberlaufen* (ist);
    — **away** weglaufen* (ist); — **over**
    überfahren* (*insep.*)
runner der Läufer, –s, –

said: be — to sollen*
sake: for the — of um (+ *gen.*) willen
salesgirl die Verkäuferin, –nen
salesman der Verkäufer, –s, –
same: the — derselbe, dieselbe, dasselbe
say sagen
scenery die Landschaft, –en

scholar der Gelehrte, –n, –n

school die Schule, –n; **to —** zur Schule, in die Schule

scientist der Wissenschaftler, –s, –

scream schreien*

second: in the — place zweitens

see sehen*

seem scheinen*

seize fassen, greifen*

sell verkaufen

semester das Semester, –s, –

send schicken, senden*

sentence der Satz, –es, ⸚e

servant der Diener, –s, –

serve dienen + *dat.*

set setzen, stellen; (*sun*) untergehen* (ist); **— the table** den Tisch decken

seventies: in the — in den siebzigern

several einige

shake hands (with) (einem) die Hand geben

sharp scharf

shine scheinen*

ship das Schiff, –es, –e

shock: have the — of his life sein blaues Wunder erleben

shoe der Schuh, –es, –e

shoot schießen*, erschießen*

short kurz

shot der Schuß, –es, ⸚e

should sollte (*subj. of* sollen)

show zeigen

shrub der Busch, –es, ⸚e

sick krank

side die Seite, –n

since *conj.* da; *prep.* seit

sing singen*

sister die Schwester, –n

sit sitzen*

sixties: in his — in den sechzigern

sleep schlafen*

slow langsam

small klein

smile das Lächeln, –s

smoke rauchen

snow der Schnee, –s

so so; **— that** so daß, damit

sold out ausverkauft

soldier der Soldat, –en, –en

some einige, manche

somebody jemand

something etwas

sometime einmal

sometimes manchmal

son der Sohn, –es, ⸚e

song der Gesang, –s, ⸚e; das Lied, –es, –er

soon bald

sound der Laut, –es, –e

south (of) südlich (+ *gen.*)

speak sprechen*

speaker der Redner, –s, –

speech die Rede, –n

spend (*money*) ausgeben*; (*time*) verbringen*

spite: in — of trotz + *gen.*

spring der Frühling, –s, –e

stand stehen*; **— up** aufstehen* (ist)

start anfangen*, beginnen*

state der Staat, –es, –en

state (*in Lesson 5 =* **write**) schreiben*

stature die Gestalt, –en

stay bleiben* (ist)

steal stehlen*

stealing das Stehlen, –s

step treten* (ist); **take a —** einen Schritt tun*

stern ernst

stick der Stock, –es, ⸚e

still noch immer

stolen gestohlen

stop = **cease** aufhören; = **halt** halten*

store der Laden, –s, ⸚

story die Geschichte, –n

strange fremd, seltsam

stranger der Fremde, –n, –n; ein Fremder

street die Straße, –n

strive streben

strong stark

student der Student, –en, –en; die Studentin, –nen

study studieren

stupid dumm

succeed: I — es gelingt* mir

successful erfolgreich

such so, solch, solcher

suddenly plötzlich, auf einmal

sufficiently genügend

summer der Sommer, –s, –

sun die Sonne, –n

Sunday der Sonntag, –s, –e

sunshine der Sonnenschein, –s

supposed: be — to sollen*

sure (of) gewiß (+ *gen.*)

surprise überraschen (*insep.*)

surprised: be — at sich wundern über + *acc.*

surround umgeben* (*insep.*)

swim schwimmen* (ist)

symphony die Symphonie, –n

table der Tisch, –es, –e

tail der Schwanz, –es, ⸚e

take nehmen*; **— along** mitnehmen*; **— away** wegnehmen*; **— a trip** eine Reise machen; **— a walk** spazierengehen* (ist), einen Spaziergang machen

talk (about) sprechen* (über + *acc.*)

tall hoch

teacher der Lehrer, –s, –; die Lehrerin, –nen

tear to pieces zerreißen*

tell = **say** sagen; = **relate** erzählen

test die Prüfung, –en; das Examen, –s, Examina

than als

that *adj.* jener, jene, jenes; *conj.* daß; *pron.* das; *rel. pron.* der, die, das; welcher, welche, welches; was

theater das Theater, –s, –

their ihr

theme der Aufsatz, –es, ⸚e

then dann

theory die Theorie, –n

there da, dort; **— is (are)** es gibt; **— are** es sind

thief der Dieb, –es, –e

thing die Sache, –n; **many a —** manches, vieles

think denken*; glauben

third dritt–

this dieser, diese, dieses

those jene; *pron.* diejenigen

thousand (das) Tausend

thrifty sparsam

through durch

thy dein

tight eng

time die Zeit; **for a long —** lange; **on —** pünktlich; **have a good —** sich amüsieren

times: many — oft; **three —** dreimal

tired müde

to zu, in + *acc.*, auf + *acc.*

today heute

tomorrow morgen; **by —** bis morgen

too (= **also**) auch; = **excessively** zu; **— much** zuviel

top der Gipfel, –s, –

toward gegen

town das Städtchen, –s, –; **to —** in die Stadt

traffic der Verkehr, –s

train der Zug, –es, ⁼e

translate übersetzen (*insep.*)

travel reisen (ist)

traveler der Reisende, –n, –n; ein Reisender

tree der Baum, –es, ⁼e

trip die Reise, –n

true wahr

tuition (**money**) das Schulgeld, –es

turn around sich umwenden*

twelfth zwölft–

two = **both** beide

twofold zweifach

umbrella der Regenschirm, –s, –e

uncle der Onkel, –s, –

under unter

understand verstehen*

United States die Vereinigten Staaten (*pl.*)

university die Universität, –en

until: not — the 21st erst am 21.

use gebrauchen, sich bedienen + *gen.*

usually gewöhnlich

vacation die Ferien (*pl.*)

vegetable(s) das Gemüse, –s, –

verb das Zeitwort, –s, ⁼er

very (**much**) sehr

vicinity die Nähe

Viennese *adj.* Wiener

view die Aussicht, –en

village das Dorf, –es, ⁼er

visit besuchen

voice die Stimme, –n

wait (**for**) warten (auf + *acc.*)

walk der Spaziergang, –s; **take a —** einen Spaziergang machen, spazierengehen* (ist)

walk gehen* (ist); **— out** hinausgehen* (ist)

wall die Wand, ⁼e

want (**to**) wollen*

war der Krieg, –es, –e

warm warm

waste verschwenden

watch die Uhr, –en

water das Wasser, –s

way (**manner**) die Weise, –n; **in no —** auf keine Weise

weak schwach

wear tragen*

weather das Wetter, –s

week die Woche, –n; **a — from today** heute über acht Tage

weekend das Wochenende, –s, –n

welcome willkommen

well gesund, wohl
well der Brunnen, –s, –
what *pron.* was; *adj.* welcher, welche,
   welches
when *interrog.* wann; *past time* als;
   = **whenever** wenn
where wo
whether ob
which *adj. and interrog. pron.* welcher,
   welche, welches; *rel. pron.* der, die, das;
   welcher, welche, welches; was
whistle pfeifen*
white weiß
who wer; *rel. pron.* der, die, das; welcher,
   welche, welches
whoever wer
whole ganz
whose *interrog.* wessen
why warum
wife die Frau, –en
wild wild
will der Wille, –ns, –n
wind der Wind, –es, –e
window das Fenster, –s, –
wine der Wein, –es, –e

with mit, bei
without ohne
wolf der Wolf, –es, ⸚e
woman die Frau, –en
woods der Wald, –es, ⸚er
word das Wort, –es, –e *and* ⸚er
work die Arbeit; arbeiten
worker der Arbeiter, –s, –
working das Arbeiten, –s
world die Welt, –en
worry (about) sich Sorgen machen (um)
worse and worse immer schlechter
worst bösest–, schlechtest–
wound verwunden
write schreiben*

yard der Hof, –es, ⸚e
year das Jahr, –es, –e
yellow gelb
yesterday gestern
young jung
your dein, euer, Ihr
yourself (*emphatic*) selbst

Zugspitze die Zugspitze

GERMAN–ENGLISH VOCABULARY

The genitive singular is given only for weak masculine nouns. Vowel changes of strong and irregular verbs are indicated, and **ist** is added where applicable. A hyphen identifies separable prefixes. **Da-** and **wo-** compounds are not listed.

ab-brechen (i), a, o break off

abends in the evening, at night

aber but, however

die Absicht, –en intention

die Achse, –n axis

achten (auf + *acc.*) pay attention (to)

der Affe, –n, –n ape, monkey

ähneln (+ *dat.*) resemble

ähnlich like, similar (to)

alle all; **trotz allem** in spite of everything; **vor allem** above all

allerlei all kinds of

allmählich gradually

als when, as; (*after comparative forms*) than; **— ob, — wenn** as if

alt old

das Alter age

der Amerikaner, – American

amüsieren amuse, entertain; **sich —** have a good time, enjoy oneself

an to, on (*vertical surfaces*), at

ander– other, different

der Anfang, ⸚e beginning; **von Anfang an** from the beginning

an-fangen (ä), i, a begin

angenehm pleasant

an-hören listen to

an-klagen (+ *gen.*) accuse (of)

an-kleiden dress

an-kommen, kam ... an, ist angekommen arrive

an-nehmen (nimmt ... an), nahm ... an, angenommen assume, accept

an-sehen (ie), a, e look at

(an)statt (+ *gen.*) instead of

der Anstreicher, – painter (*of walls, buildings, etc.*)

antworten answer

an-ziehen: sich —, zog ... an, angezogen dress (oneself)

der Anzug, ⸚e suit

die Arbeit, –en work, piece of work

arbeiten work

arg bad, severe

ärgern annoy, make angry, irritate; **sich —** get angry, be annoyed

arm poor

der Arm, –e arm

die Armee, –n army

die Art, –en sort, kind; manner

der Arzt, ⸚e physician, doctor

der Ast, ⸚e limb, branch

auch also, too

auf on (*horizontal surfaces*), in, upon, at, to; **— einmal** suddenly, all at once; **aufs neue** again, anew

auf-bauen develop

die Aufgabe, –n lesson

auf-nehmen (nimmt ... auf), nahm ... auf, aufgenommen admit, receive; take a photograph of; absorb

auf-passen pay attention, look out

der Aufsatz, ⸚e theme

auf-stehen, stand auf, ist aufgestanden get up

das Auge, –n eye

aus (+ *dat.*) out, out of, from

aus-nehmen (nimmt ... aus), nahm ... aus, ausgenommen take out; except

aus-ruhen: sich — have a good rest

aus-sehen (ie), a, e look, appear

der Außenminister, – secretary of state, foreign minister

außer (+ *dat.*) besides, except

außerhalb (+ *gen.*) outside (of)

äußerst extremely, most

aus-steigen, ie, ie (ist) get off, get out

aus-ziehen: sich —, zog ... aus, ausgezogen undress

das Auto, –s automobile

der Autobus, –se bus

backen (ä), buk, gebacken bake

baden bathe

der Bahnhof, ⸚e railroad station

bald soon

das Band, –e tie, bond

das Band, ⸚er ribbon

der Band, ⸚e volume, book

die Bande troop, gang

bauen build

der Bauer, –s *or* **–n, –n** farmer

der Baum, ⸚e tree

beantworten answer

beben tremble, shake

bedanken: sich — express thanks

bedeuten mean

bedienen: sich — (+ *gen.*) use, make use of, avail oneself of

bedürfen (bedarf), bedurfte, bedurft (+ *gen.*) need, have need of, require, want

bedürftig needy, in need of

beeilen: sich — hurry, hasten

befehlen (ie), a, o command

befinden: sich —, a, u find oneself, be

befreien liberate

befürchten fear

begegnen (+ *dat.*) (**ist**) meet

beginnen, a, o begin

behalten (**ä**), **ie, a** keep

bei (+ *dat.*) near, at the home (office) of, in (*weather*), while (*doing something*); — **weitem** by far

beide both

das Bein, –e leg

beißen, biß, gebissen bite

bei-wohnen (+ *dat.*) attend, be present at

bekannt known, familiar

der Bekannte, –n; ein Bekannter acquaintance

bekommen, bekam, bekommen get, receive

die Belohnung, –en reward

bemächtigen: sich — (+ *gen.*) take possession of

bemerken notice, observe

benehmen: sich — (**benimmt**), **benahm, benommen** behave

beobachten watch, observe

bequem comfortable

bereisen travel through, visit

der Berg, –e mountain

berichten report

berufen, ie, u call; appoint

berühmt famous

beschuldigen (+ *gen.*) accuse of

besser better

bestehen (**auf** + *dat.*), **bestand, bestanden** insist on

bestellen order

bestens as well as possible

der Besuch, –e visit

besuchen visit, call on; attend, go to

betragen (**ä**), **u, a** amount to; **sich —** behave

das Bett, –en bed

bewegen move

beweisen, ie, ie prove, demonstrate

bewerben: sich — um (**i**), **a, o** apply for

bewußt conscious, aware (of)

bezahlen pay

die Bibliothek, –en library

das Bier, –e beer

das Bild, –er picture

die Binde, –n bandage, string

binden, a, u tie, bind

die Biographie, –n biography

bis (+ *acc.*) (up) to, until; — **jetzt** up to now

bitten, bat, gebeten ask for, request

blaß pale

das Blatt, ⸚er leaf

bleiben, ie, ie (**ist**) stay, remain

der Bleistift, –e pencil

die Blume, –n flower

der Boden, – *or* ⸚ floor

böse (+ *dat.*) angry (with)

der Bote, –n messenger

braten (**ä**), **ie, a** roast, fry

brauchen need, use

braun brown

die Braut, ⸚e fiancée

brechen (**i**), **a, o** break

brennen, brannte, gebrannt burn

der Brief, –e letter

der Briefträger, – postman

bringen, brachte, gebracht bring

das Brot, –e bread

der Bruder, ⸚ brother

das Buch, ⸚er book

das Büchlein, – little book

bücken: sich — bend down, stoop

das Bund, –e bundle, bunch (of keys)

der Bund, ⁼e band; alliance

das Büro, –s office

da *adv.* there, then; *conj.* since, because

das Dach, ⁼er roof

damit *conj.* that, so that, in order that

der Dank thanks, gratitude; **vielen —** many thanks, thanks very much

dankbar grateful

danken (+ *dat.*) thank

dann then

daß *conj.* that, so that

dauern last, continue

dein your

deinetwegen for your sake

denken, dachte, gedacht think

der, die, das; (*pl.*) **die** *def. art.* the; *dem. adj.* that, those; *dem. pron.* that, that one, he, she, it; those, they; *rel. pron.* who, that, which

derjenige, diejenige, dasjenige that, that one, the one

derselbe, dieselbe, dasselbe the same, the same one

(das) Deutsch German (language)

(das) Deutschland Germany

der Dezember December

der Dichter, – poet

dichterisch poetic

der Dieb, –e thief

dienen (+ *dat.*) serve

der Diener, – servant

dieser, diese, dieses this; the latter

diesseits (+ *gen.*) on this side of

der Direktor, –en director

doch however, still, after all, yet (on the other hand)

der Doktor, –en doctor, Ph.D.

der Dollar, –s dollar

donnern thunder

drehen turn, rotate; **sich —** revolve

dringen, a, u (**ist**) penetrate, press forward

drohen (+ *dat.*) threaten

drucken print

dumm stupid

der Dummkopf, ⁼e blockhead, simpleton

dunkel dark

durch (+ *acc.*) through, by means of

durchaus extremely, most

dürfen (darf), durfte, gedurft be allowed to, may; **nicht —** must not

die Ecke, –n corner

edel noble

ehe *conj.* before

eher ... als more . . . than

die Ehre, –n honor

eigen own

einander each other, one another

ein-bilden: sich (*dat.*) **—** imagine

ein-fallen (fällt ... ein), fiel ... ein, ist eingefallen occur (to one's mind)

einige some

die Einkünfte *f. pl.* income

einmal once; **auf —** all at once

ein-steigen, ie, ie (**ist**) get in, board

ein-treten (tritt ... ein), trat ... ein, ist eingetreten enter, come in

der Elefant, –en, –en elephant

die Eltern *pl.* parents

empfangen (ä), i, a receive

empfehlen (ie), a, o recommend

das Ende, –n end

endlich finally, at last

entdecken discover

entfliehen (+ dat.), o, o (ist) flee, escape
(from)

entgehen, entging, ist entgangen escape (from)

entkommen (+ dat.), entkam, ist entkommen escape (from)

entlang along

entlaufen (äu), ie, au (ist) escape

entscheiden: sich —, ie, ie decide

entsprechen (+ dat.) (i), a, o corre-
spond to

entstehen, entstand, ist entstanden
originate, arise

die Entstehung, –en origin

entwickeln develop

die Erde, –n earth

erfahren (ä), u, a experience

die Erfahrung, –en experience

erfolgen result, follow

erfreuen please

erheben exalt, raise

erholen: sich — (von + dat.) recover
(from)

erinnern (an + acc.) remind of; sich —
(+ gen. or an + acc.) remember

erkälten: sich — catch a cold

erklären explain, declare

erkundigen: sich — (nach) inquire
(about)

erst first; only, not until

erzählen relate, tell

essen (ißt), aß, gegessen eat

etliche some

etwas something; somewhat; noch —
something else

euer your

(das) Europa Europe

die Fabrik, –en factory

fähig (+ gen. or zu) capable (of)

die Fahne, –n flag

fahren (ä), u, a (ist) ride, drive, go,
travel

fallen (fällt), fiel, ist gefallen fall

fällen fell, cut down

fangen (ä), i, a catch

fast almost

faul lazy

der Februar February

die Feder, –n pen

fehlen (+ dat.) be lacking, be missing

fein fine, delicate, nice

der Feind, –e enemy

feindlich (+ dat.) hostile (toward)

das Feld, –er field

das Fenster, – window

die Ferien pl. vacation, holidays

der Film, –e film, movie

finden, a, u find

flattern flutter, fly (of hair, flags, etc.)

das Fleisch meat

fleißig diligent, hard

fliegen, o, o (ist) fly

fliehen, o, o (ist) flee, run

fließen, floß, ist geflossen flow

fluchen curse, swear

die Flucht, –en flight, escape

der Flug, ⸗e flight

das Flugzeug, –e airplane

der Fluß, ⸗e river

folgen (+ *dat.*) (**ist**) follow

fort-fahren (**ä**), **u, a** (**ist**) drive away

die Frage, –n question; **eine — stellen** ask a question

fragen ask

die Fraktur Gothic type

der Franzose, –n, –n Frenchman

die Französin, –nen Frenchwoman

die Frau, –en woman; wife; Mrs.

das Fräulein, – young lady; Miss

die Freiheit, –en freedom

fremd (+ *dat.*) strange (to)

fressen (**frißt**), **fraß, gefressen** eat (*animals*)

die Freude, –n joy, pleasure

freuen please; **sich —** (+ *gen.*) be pleased (with), be glad (of); **sich — auf** + *acc.* look forward to; **sich — über** + *acc.* rejoice at, be pleased with

der Freund, –e friend

die Freundin, –nen friend

freundlich friendly, kind

der Friede, –ns, –n peace

froh happy, merry, glad

fromm pious

früh early

frühestens as early as possible; at the earliest, not before

der Frühling, –e spring

das Frühstück, –e breakfast; **zum —** for breakfast

fühlen feel; **sich —** feel

führen lead, guide

für (+ *acc.*) for, in return for

furchtbar terrible

fürchten fear; **sich —** (**vor** + *dat.*) be afraid (of)

der Fuß, ̈e foot; **zu — gehen** walk

ganz entire, whole

das Gebäude, – building

geben (**i**), **a, e** give; **es gibt** there is, there are

gebieten, o, o order, command

gebräuchlich usable, in use

der Gedanke, –ns, –n thought

gedenken, gedachte, gedacht (+ *gen.*) remember, think of

das Gedicht, –e poem

gefallen (**gefällt**), **gefiel, gefallen** (+ *dat.*) please, be pleasing (to)

der Gefangene, –n, –n prisoner

das Gefängnis, –se prison

gegen (+ *acc.*) toward, against, in return for, in comparison with

das Gehalt, ̈er salary

gehen, ging, ist gegangen go, walk

gehorchen (+ *dat.*) obey

gehören (+ *dat.*) belong to

der Geist, –er spirit

das Geld, –er money

gelingen, a, u (**ist**) (+ *dat.*) succeed, be successful (for)

das Gemach, ̈er room

das Gemälde, – painting

genug enough

genügen (+ *dat.*) suffice, be sufficient (for)

das Gepäck, –e baggage

gerade just, just now, just then; straight

geradeaus straight ahead

das Gericht, –e court

gern(e) gladly; (*with any verb*) like to

geschehen (**ie**), **a, e** (**ist**) happen

die Geschichte, –n story, history

das Geschirr, –e dishes

das Gesetz, –e law

das Gesicht, –e vision

das Gesicht, –er face

gestalten form, shape

gestern yesterday

gesund well, healthy

gewinnen, a, o win

gewiß (+ *gen.*) certain, sure (of)

gewöhnen: sich — (**an** + *acc.*) become accustomed (to)

gewohnt used to, accustomed to

glänzen glitter

das Glas, ⁼er glass

glatt smooth

der Glaube, –ns, –n belief

glauben believe, think

gleich (+ *dat.*) equal, similar (to)

gleichen, i, i (+ *dat.*) (be) equal (to), resemble

das Glück luck, good fortune; **zum —** luckily, fortunately

glücklich happy, lucky; safe

das Gold gold

golden gold, of gold

das Golf golf

der Gott, ⁼er God, god

graben (ä), u, a dig

gratulieren (+ *dat.*) (**zu etwas**) congratulate (on something)

greifen, i, i grasp

grob coarse, rude

groß large, big; great; tall

der Großvater, ⁼ grandfather

grün green

grüßen greet

gut good, well

das Haar, –e hair

haben (hat), hatte, gehabt have

halb half

die Hälfte, –n half

halten (ä), ie, a hold, stop

der Hammer, ⁼ hammer

die Hand, ⁼e hand

hängen, i, a hang

hart harsh, severe; hard

das Haupt, ⁼er head

das Haus, ⁼er house; **nach Hause** home; **zu Hause** at home

heben, o, o lift

heilen cure

das Heilmittel, – medicine, remedy

die Heimat home

heim-suchen afflict

heiß hot

heißen, ie, ei be called, be named

helfen (i), a, o (+ *dat.*) help

hell bright

her here (*toward the speaker*); **hin und her** back and forth

herein in (here)

herein-kommen, kam ... herein, ist hereingekommen come in

der Herr, –n, –en gentleman; Mr.; master

die Herrschaft rule

herrschen rule

herum around

hervorragend outstanding

das Herz, –ens, –en heart

das Herzogtum, ⁼er duchy

heute today; **von — an** from today on

heutig– today's, of today

hier here; **von — aus** from here

die Hilfe help, assistance

hin there (*away from speaker*); **— und her** back and forth

hinaus out
hinein in (there)
hinter behind
hinüber-setzen take across
hoch high; tall
höchst extremely, most, very
höchstens at most, at best
hold gracious
holen fetch, go and get
das Holz, ⁼er wood
hören hear
der Hügel, – hill
der Hund, –e dog
der Hut, ⁼e hat

die Idee, –n idea
ihr her, its, their
Ihr your
immer always
in in, into
inner inner, interior
innerhalb (+ *gen.*) inside (of)
interessant interesting
interessieren interest; **sich — (für)**
  be(come) interested (in)
der Irrtum, ⁼er error

das Jahr, –e year
der Januar January
je ... desto the . . . the
jeder, jede, jedes each, every
jedermann everybody
jemand someone, anyone
jener, jene, jenes that; the former
jenseits (+ *gen.*) on the other side of
jetzt now; **bis —** up to now; **von — an**
  from now on

die Jugend youth, young people; **von —**
  auf from (my, his, etc.) youth (on)
der Juli July
jung young
der Junge, –n, –n boy

der Kaffee, –s coffee
kalt cold
der Kamin, –e fireplace
kämpfen fight
das Kapitel, – chapter
die Kartoffel, –n potato
der Käse, – cheese
das Kästchen, – little box
das Kätzchen, – kitten
die Katze, –n cat
kaufen buy, purchase
kein, keine, kein no, not a, not any
kennen, kannte, gekannt be acquainted
  with, know
das Kind, –er child
das Kino, –s movies, movie theater
die Kirche, –n church
das Kirchenfenster, — church window
klar clear
die Klasse, –n class
das Klassenzimmer, — classroom
das Klavier, –e piano
das Klavierspielen playing the piano
das Kleid, –er dress
kleiden dress, clothe
klettern climb
klingen, a, u sound
klug clever
der Knecht, –e servant
komisch funny
kommen, kam, ist gekommen come

kompliziert complex

der König, –e king

die Königin, –nen queen

können (kann), konnte, gekonnt be able to, can; may (*possibility*); know (have acquired knowledge of), know how to

der Kopf, ⁼e head

der Kopfschmerz, –en headache

kosten cost

krank sick, ill

der Kranke, –n, –n sick person, patient

kreisen orbit, revolve

kriechen, o, o (ist) crawl, creep

krumm crooked

die Kuh, ⁼e cow

kümmern: sich — (um) worry (about)

das Kunstwerk, –e work of art

kurz short; **seit kurzem** recently, not long ago

lächeln smile

lachen laugh

laden (lädt), lud, geladen load

das Land, ⁼er land, country

die Landschaft landscape

lang long; **einen Monat —** for a month

längst *adv.* long

lassen (läßt), ließ, gelassen permit, let

lasten weigh upon, press heavily upon

laufen (äu), ie, au (ist) run

die Laune, –n mood

laut loud

das Leben life

leben live

leer empty

legen lay, put

lehnen lean

lehren teach

der Lehrer, – teacher

leicht light, easy

leid tun, a, a: es tut mir leid I am sorry

leiden, litt, gelitten suffer

leihen, ie, ie lend

leisten: zu leistende Zahlungen time payments; **sich (*dat.*) leisten** afford

die Leiter, –n ladder

lernen learn

lesen (ie), a, e pick, gather; read, lecture

letzt– last

die Leute *pl.* people

lieb dear

lieben love, like

lieber (+ *verb*) rather, prefer to (*comparative of* **gern**)

liegen, a, e lie, be situated

lila lilac, violet

der Löffel, – spoon

los loose; free; **etwas — sein** be rid of something; **etwas — werden** get rid of something

löschen extinguish, blot out

der Löwe, –n, –n lion

lügen, o, o tell a lie

lustig amusing, merry

machen make, do

mächtig strong, powerful; **— sein** (*gen.*) have mastery of

das Mädchen, – girl

der Mai May

malen paint

der Maler painter

man one, they, you, people

mancher, manche, manches many a; *pl.* some

mancherlei many kinds of

manchmal sometimes

der Mann, ⸚er man

die Mark mark (*unit of currency*)

der Markt, ⸚e market, market place

die Masern *pl.* measles

die Mauer, –n wall

die Medizin, –en medicine

mehr more

mehrere several

die Meile, –n mile

mein, my; **meiner, der meinige, der meine** mine

meinen mean (to say), think, believe

meinetwegen for my sake

die Meinigen my own (people, family)

die Meinung, –en opinion; **meiner — nach** in my opinion

meist– most

meistens usually, mostly, as a rule

die Menge, –n crowd

der Mensch, –en, –en person, human being; *pl.* people

messen (mißt), maß, gemessen measure

die Milch milk

mit (+ *dat.*) with, by means of

mit-bringen, brachte mit, mitgebracht bring along

mit-nehmen (nimmt ... mit), nahm ... mit, mitgenommen take along

das Mittagessen lunch, dinner; **zum —** for lunch

mittags at noon; at lunch time

das Mittel, – means (*to any end; hence, medicine, anesthetic, etc.*)

mitten in the middle

die Mitternacht, ⸚e midnight

mögen (mag), mochte, gemocht like to; may (*possibility*)

möglich possible

möglichst (bald, etc.) as (soon) as possible

der Monat, –e month

der Montag, –e Monday

der Morgen, – morning

morgen tomorrow

morgens in the morning

müde (+ *gen.*) tired (of)

die Mühe, –n trouble; **— machen** cause trouble; **sich mühen** take pains *or* trouble

(das) München Munich

der Muselman, –en, –en Moslem

müssen (muß), mußte, gemußt have to, must

die Mutter, ⸚ mother

nach (+ *dat.*) to, after, toward, according to; **— vorn** forward, to the front

der Nachbar, –s *or* **–n, –n** neighbor

nachdem *conj.* after

nachmittags in the afternoon

nächst– next

die Nacht, ⸚e night

nachts at night

der Nagel, ⸚ nail

nah near, close

nähern: sich — (+ *dat.*) approach

der Name, –ns, –n name

naß wet

neben near, next to, beside(s)

der Neffe, –n, –n nephew

nehmen (nimmt), nahm, genommen take

nein no

nennen, nannte, genannt call, name, mention

neu new; **aufs neue** again, anew

nicht not

nichts nothing

das Nichtsein not to be

niemand nobody

noch yet, still, more, in addition; **— ein** one more; **— etwas** something (anything) else; **— nicht** not yet

nördlich (+ *gen.*) north (of)

nun now; **von — an** from now on

nur only, just

nützen (+ *dat.*) be useful (to)

nützlich useful

ob if, whether

oberhalb (+ *gen.*) above

offen open

öffnen open

oft often

ohne (+ *acc.*) without

das Ohr, –en ear

der Onkel, – uncle

der Ort, –e *or* **–er** place, locality

(die) Ostern Easter

östlich (+ *gen.*) east (of)

paar: ein — a few, a couple

das Paar, –e pair

das Papier, –e paper

der Park, –e park

passen (+ *dat.*) (be) fit, suit

pfeifen, pfiff, gepfiffen whistle

das Pferd, –e horse

pflanzen plant

pflegen care for; nurse

das Pfund, –e pound

der Philosoph, –en, –en philosopher

der Platz, –̈e place, space

die Politik politics, policy

die Polizei police

die Post post office; mail

der Preis, –e price; prize

preisen, ie, ie praise

der Preuße, –n, –n Prussian

(das) Preußen Prussia

der Professor, –en professor

die Prüfung, –en examination, test

quellen (i), o, o (ist) gush, flow

die Quittung, –en receipt

das Radio, –s radio

raten (ä), ie, a advise

das Rätsel, – puzzle

rauben rob

rauchen smoke

räuspern: sich — clear one's throat

das Rechnen figuring, arithmetic

recht (+ *dat.*) (all) right, agreeable (to); **— haben** to be right

reden speak, talk

der Regen, – rain

die Regierung, –en government

regnen rain

reich rich

die Reise, –n trip, journey

reisen (ist) travel

der Reisende, –n, –n; ein Reisender traveler

reißen, riß, gerissen tear

reiten, ritt, ist geritten ride (on horseback)

reizend charming

die Reklame, –n advertisement

rennen, rannte, ist gerannt run

die Résistance resistance

das Restaurant, –s restaurant

retten rescue

der Richter, – judge

der Ring, –e ring

der Roman, –e novel

rosa rose

rot red

rufen, ie, u call

rühmen: sich — (+ *gen.*) boast (of)

rund round

die Sache, –n matter, affair, thing

der Sachse, –n Saxon

sagen say, tell

sammeln gather

der Sänger, – singer

schaden (+ *dat.*) harm

der Schaden, ≐ damage

der Schaffner, – conductor

schämen: sich — (+ *gen.*, **wegen +** *gen., or* **über +** *acc.*) be ashamed (of)

scharf sharp

schauen see, gaze (upon), view

scheinen, ie, ie shine; seem

schelten (i), a, o to scold, call (*an uncomplimentary name*)

scheren shear, clip

schicken send

das Schicksal, –e destiny, fate

schimpfen scold, abuse, call (*an uncomplimentary name*)

schlafen (ä), ie, a sleep

schlagen (ä), u, a hit, strike

der Schlager, – hit (*popular book, song, play*)

schlecht bad

schließen, schloß, geschlossen close, lock

schlimm bad

schlingen, a, u entwine, tie

das Schloß, ≐er castle, palace; lock

schmal narrow

schmecken (+ *dat.*) taste, taste good (to)

schmeicheln (+ *dat.*) flatter

schmeißen, schmiß, geschmissen hurl, throw

schmelzen (i), o, o (ist) melt, fuse

schmerzen hurt, pain, grieve

schneiden, schnitt, geschnitten cut

schnell fast, quick

schon already, all right

schön beautiful, nice, fine

die Schönheit, –en beauty

schrauben screw

schrecken (schrickt), schrak, ist geschrocken be frightened

schreiben, ie, ie write

die Schreibmaschine, –n typewriter

der Schreibtisch, –e desk

schreien, ie, ie scream

schreiten, schritt, ist geschritten step

der Schuh, –e shoe

schuldig guilty

die Schule, –n school

der Schutzmann, *pl.* **Schutzleute** policeman

schwach weak

schwarz black

die Schweiz Switzerland

schwer heavy, difficult

die Schwester, –n sister

schwimmen, a, o (ist) swim, float

sehen (ie), a, e see

sehnen: sich — (nach) long (for)

sehr very (much)

die Seide, –n silk

sein (ist), war, ist gewesen be

das Sein to be, being

sein, seine, sein his, its

seit (+ dat.) since, for (duration of time);
— drei Jahren for three years; —
kurzem recently, not long ago;
— wann since when

selber, selbst (intensive pron.) –self,
–selves; ich selber I myself

selbst adv. even

das Semester, – semester

senden, sandte, gesandt send

der September September

setzen set, put, place; sich — sit down,
take a seat

sich himself, herself, itself, themselves,
yourself, yourselves

sicher safe, sure (of)

singen, a, u sing

sinnen, a, o think

sitzen, saß, gesessen sit

so so, thus, this way, that way, then;
so ... wie as . . . as

das Sofa, –s sofa

der Sohn, ⸗e son

solcher, solche, solches such (a)

sollen (soll), sollte, gesollt be supposed
to, be to, shall

der Sommer, – summer

die Sommerwoche, –n summer week,
week in summer

die Sonne, –n sun

der Sonntag, –e Sunday

spalten split

spät late; Wie — ist es? What time
is it?

spätestens at the latest

der Spaziergang, ⸗e walk, stroll; einen
— machen take a walk

der Speisewagen, – dining car

der Sperling, –e sparrow

der Spiegel, – mirror

spielen play, act

spinnen, a, o spin

sprechen (i), a, o talk, speak

der Staat, –en state, country

die Stadt, ⸗e city

stark strong

statt (+ gen.) instead of

stecken be; stick, put

stehen, stand, gestanden stand

steigen, ie, ie (ist) climb

stellen place, put

die Stellung, –en job, position

sterben (i), a, o (ist) die

der Stern, –e star

die Stimme, –n voice

der Stoff, –e material, fabric

stolz proud

stoßen (ö), ie, o push

der Strand, –e beach

die Straße, –n street

streichen, i, i stroke

der Strom electricity

der Student, –en, –en student

die Studentin, –nen student

studieren study

der Stuhl, ⸗e chair

die Stunde, –n hour

stürzen destroy

suchen look for, seek

südlich (+ *gen.*) south (of)
die Suppe, –n soup

der Tag, –e day
tanzen dance
die Tasche, –n pocket
die Tasse, –n cup
tasten: sich — feel one's way
die Tatsache, –n fact
taufen christen, baptize
der Teich, –e pool
teilen divide
teuer dear, expensive
der Text, –e text; words
das Theater, – theater
das Tier, –e animal
der Tisch, –e table
das Tischbein, –e table leg
die Tochter, ⸗ daughter
der Tod death
der Ton, ⸗e sound, tone
tragen (ä), u, a carry, bear
trauen (+ *dat.*) trust
treiben, ie, ie drive
treten (tritt), trat, ist getreten step,
  walk
treu faithful, true
trinken, a, u drink
trotz (+ *gen.*) in spite of; — allem in
  spite of everything
tun, tat, getan do
die Tür, –en door
der Türgriff, –e doorknob

üben: sich — (in) practice
über over, above; about (concerning)
überaus extremely, most
überraschend surprising

übersetzen translate
die Übersiedlung, –en moving
die Uhr, –en clock, watch; ein — one
  o'clock; **Wieviel — ist es?** What time
  is it?
um (+ *acc.*) around, at (*time by clock*);
  — (+ *gen.*) willen for the sake of;
  — seinetwillen for his sake
um-drehen turn around
umstehen, umstand, umstanden stand
  around or about, surround
unbekannt unknown
(das) Ungarn Hungary
der Unglückliche, –en, –en unfortu-
  nate person
die Universität, –en university
unmöglich impossible
unschuldig innocent
unser our
unter under; among
unterhalb (+ *gen.*) below
unterhalten (ä), ie, a entertain
unterscheiden, ie, ie distinguish, differ-
  entiate
urteilen judge, pass sentence

der Vater, ⸗ father
verändern change
verbeugen: sich — bow
verbieten, o, o forbid, prohibit
verbinden, a, u tie, bind; bandage,
  dress (*wound*)
verbrennen burn
verdächtig (+ *gen.*) suspected (of)
verfallen (verfällt) verfiel, ist verfallen decay, decline
verhören examine, interrogate
verirren: sich — lose one's way

verkehren come and go, frequent, visit

verlassen (verläßt), verließ, verlassen leave; **sich —** (**auf** + *acc.*) depend (on)

verlieren, o, o lose

veröffentlichen publish

versprechen (i), a, o promise

der Verstand understanding

verständlich intelligible

verstehen, verstand, verstanden understand

verstoßen (ö), ie, o offend, transgress

versuchen attempt, try

vertragen: sich — (**ä**)**, u, a** agree

verwandt related

der Vetter, –n cousin

verweisen, ie, ie reprimand, rebuke

viel much; **viele** *pl.* many

vielerlei many kinds of

die Violine, –n violin

der Vogel, ÷ bird

voll full

von (+ *dat.*) by, from, of, about; **— Anfang an** from the beginning; **— heute an** from today on; **—hier aus** from here; **— jetzt an** from now on; **— Jugend auf** from (my, his, etc.) youth (on)

vor before, in front of; **— einem Monat** a month ago; **— allem** above all; **— sich hin** to himself

voran-gehen, ging ... voran, ist vorangegangen precede

vor-lesen (ie), a, e lecture, read aloud

vormittags in the forenoon, in the morning

vorn in front; **nach —** forward, to the front

vor-stellen introduce, present; **sich** (*dat.*) **—** imagine

wachsen (ä), u, a (ist) grow

der Wagen, – car, automobile

wahr true, real

während (+ *gen.*) during; *conj.* while

die Wahrheit, –en truth

der Wald, ÷er forest

die Wand, ÷e wall

die Wandtafel, –n blackboard

wann when; **seit —** since when

warm warm

warten wait; look after, attend (to), nurse

was what; **— für ein** what kind of, what (a)

waschen (ä), u, a wash; **sich —** wash (oneself)

die Wasserfarbe, –n water color

wecken wake, awaken

der Weg, –e way, road, path

wegen (+ *gen.*) on account of

weh painful, sore

weh tun (+ *dat.*) hurt

Weihnachten Christmas

der Wein, –e wine

das Weinen weeping

weiß white

weit far, distant; **bei weitem** by far

weiter farther, further

welcher, welche, welches *interrog.* which, what (a); *rel. pron.* who, which, that

die Weltmacht, ÷e world power

wenden, wandte, gewandt turn

wenig little

wenigstens at least

wenn, if, when, whenever

wer who, whoever, he who

werden (wird), wurde, ist geworden become, get (to be)

werfen (i), a, o throw

wessen (*gen. of* **wer**) whose

westlich (+ *gen.*) west (of)

wetten bet, wager

das Wetter, – weather

wichtig important

wider (+ *acc.*) against (*in the sense of resistance or opposition*)

widerhallen echo

widersprechen (i), a, o (+ *dat.*) contradict

wie as; how

wieder again

wieder-entdecken rediscover

wieder-holen go and get again

wiegen, o, o weigh; **sich wiegen** (*weak*) rock, move to and fro

wieviel how much; **Wieviel Uhr ist es?** What time is it?; **der wievielte** what date

der Wille, –ns, –n will

willkommen welcome

der Wind, –e wind

winken wave; beckon; make signs

der Winter, – winter

wissen (weiß), wußte, gewußt know (*factual information*)

der Wissenschaftler, – scientist

wo where

die Woche, –n week

woher from where, where . . . from

wohin where (to what place)

wohl well, indeed, presumably, probably

wohnen live, reside, dwell

wollen (will), wollte, gewollt want (to)

das Wort, –e words (*in context*); **das Wort, ⸚er** (*separate*) words

das Wörterbuch, ⸚er dictionary

wundern: sich — (**über** + *acc.*) be surprised (at)

wünschen wish, want

würdig (+ *gen.*) worthy (of)

würfeln throw dice

zählen count

die Zahlung, –en payment

der Zahnarzt. ⸚e dentist

zaubern do by magic; practice magic

zeigen show

die Zeit, –en time

die Zeitung, –en newspaper

zerbrechen (i), a, o break

zerreißen, zerriß, zerrissen tear to bits

das Zeug, –e tool

ziehen, zog, gezogen pull

das Zimmer, – room

zu (+ *dat.*) to, at; *adv.* too

zu-machen close

zurück-kehren (ist) return, go back

der Zuschauer, – onlooker, spectator

zuviel too much

zuweilen sometimes

der Zweifel, – doubt

zwischen between

INDEX